REFRESHING THE PARTS

Refreshing the Parts
Electoral Reform and British Politics

edited by
Gareth Smyth

LAWRENCE & WISHART
LONDON

Lawrence & Wishart Ltd
144a Old South Lambeth Road
London SW8 1XX

ISBN 0 85315 753 7

First published 1992

Text and cover design by Jan Brown Designs
Photoset in North Wales by
Derek Doyle and Associates, Mold, Clwyd
Printed and bound in Great Britain by
Dotesios, Trowbridge

CONTENTS

v

CONTENTS

INTRODUCTION

'For too long the subject has been the preserve of the Liberal Democrats and the flat-earthers. It is time for a national debate.' This observation in a *Financial Times* leader (12 July 1991), while gently reflecting a wide prejudice about electoral reform, registered unequivocally that the issue was back on the agenda.

It already seems strange to think it ever went away. Britain's electoral system is not cast in stone. Profound changes have been thought necessary from time to time. The numbers of men allowed to vote increased gradually during the last century. Women received the vote on equal terms with men in 1928, and eighteen to twenty year-olds were enfranchised in 1969. Voting was made secret in 1873, and in 1911 MPs became salaried (£400 a year). In 1969 candidates were allowed six words on the ballot paper to describe their political affiliations – the official fiction that only the candidate's name counted was laid to rest.

Until 1885 less than half of constituencies had only one Member of Parliament, and it is only since 1950 that all Westminster constituencies have been single-member. The abolition of First-Past-the-Post was widely mooted in the first third of the twentieth century. In 1910 a Royal Commission supported proportional representation, and in 1917 a Speaker's Conference backed the Alternative Vote.

Further unsuccessful attempts at reform were made in 1918 and 1930: on the latter occasion the House of Lords sabotaged a bill backed by the Labour Government and the Liberals to introduce the Alternative Vote. In more modern times the Single Transferable Vote was introduced in 1973 for Assembly and local government elections in Northern Ireland, and then extended to European Parliament elections in the province. In 1977, a Commons majority of only ninety-seven prevented the introduction of PR for Euro-elections for the UK as a whole. First-Past-the-Post was taken for granted when two major parties predominated. In 1945 Labour and the Conservatives won 88 per cent of the overall vote, and over 96 per cent in both 1951 and 1955. But by February 1974 their joint share had

vii

declined to 75 per cent, and reached a post war low of 70 per cent in 1983. February 1974 produced the first hung Parliament for over forty years. 1983 was the first genuinely three-cornered general election since 1923, but when the Liberal/SDP Alliance won only 23 seats with over a quarter of the vote the 'fairness' of the system was inevitably questioned. Cries of 'foul' were repeated after the 1989 Euro-elections when three million people voted for the Greens, who ended up without a single Euro-MP.

In the 1940s and 1950s general election were won by parties with around half the overall vote: in 1945 Labour took 48 per cent, the Conservatives a shade below 50 per cent in 1955 and over 49 per cent in 1959. The share of the winning party was down to less than 40 per cent for Labour in October 1974, and under Margaret Thatcher the Conservatives spent eleven years using substantial parliamentary majorities to implement a radical programme without ever winning more than 44 per cent.

The emergence of a third-party challenge produced more constituencies won on less than half the vote. Scotland by the 1970s had a four-party system, and by 1987 tactical voting was rife. Off to the scrapheap went Professor Robert MacKenzie's 'swingometer' – a simple mechanical device which predicted the composition of the Commons on the basis of the swing between the major parties.

Simultaneously, the number of safe seats under First-Past-the-Post increased, concentrating the energies and resources of the parties in a dwindling number of 'marginals'. Critics of First-Past-the-Post were able to argue that votes outside the marginals were largely 'wasted'.

Demographic changes coupled with increasing regional variations in voting behaviour led to a growing divide between Labour seats in the inner cities, industrial towns and the north, and Conservative predominance in the south of England. Popular awareness of a 'north/south' divide heightened under the Thatcher Governments, a divide emphasised by the electoral system. In 1987 Labour won 1.7 million votes yet only three parliamentary seats outside London south of a line from the Wash to the Severn Estuary.

The growing integration of the European Community, which Britain had joined in 1973, led to comparisons with other European countries. Underlying politics since at least the 1960s has been a growing sense of Britain's relative decline, particularly with regard to its immediate European neighbours. Labour's campaign for the 1989 European Assembly elections found growing interest in pension levels,

Matt. © *The Daily Telegraph* plc, September 1991. Reproduced by kind permission.

maternity rights, and training in other EC states: it became commonplace to compare, usually adversely, Britain's railways with German and French railways, and even Britain's drinking water was suddenly no longer 'the safest in the world'. The political system could not remain immune from comparison and inspection.

Catalyst to the re-emergence of electoral reform as a political issue has been the end of a bipartisan approach dating back to the early 1930s. Support for electoral reform made rapid headway within the Labour Party after its third successive defeat in 1987, and by the October 1990 conference Labour's increasingly open approach was marked by the establishment of a committee of enquiry under Professor Raymond Plant. A subject previously dismissed by commentators as a 'fad' of the Liberal Democrats and Charter 88 suddenly had to be treated seriously.

Refreshing the Parts offers the first overall analysis of the re-emergence of the reform issue in British politics. David Marquand concisely outlines the basic case for change in terms not just of 'justice' and 'democracy' but of the basic health of the system. Political competition refreshes the parts.

Helena Catt offers a lucid guide to alternative electoral systems, and provides a 'consumer's guide to voting systems' to enable readers to choose one off the shelf. Judgments have to be made about the value of strict proportionality (arguably ensured only through a party list system), the link of the MP to constituents, the relative benefits of single-party and coalition government, and the kind of choice offered to the voter on the ballot paper. Practising politicians Peter Hain, Jeff Rooker and Robin Squire make the case for their favoured systems – the alternative vote, the additional member system and the single transferable vote respectively.

Evidence from opinion polls has played an important part in the resurgence of media coverage of electoral reform. Politicians' ears perk up if votes are at stake. But while some commentators have suggested electoral reform is a potential vote-winner, others have dismissed it as the concern of the 'chattering classes'. I look at the evidence.

The Scottish Constitutional Convention for a long time escaped the attention of London-based commentators, despite the reduction of the Conservatives to ten out of seventy-two parliamentary seats in 1987. A fast-developing situation reflects the specific politics north of the border, yet at the same time may offer a wider model of sustained cross-party co-operation. Peter Jones puts 'The Scottish Experience in Proportion'.

Nina Fishman argues that the retention of a First-Past-the-Post system has resulted from the failure of electoral reformers to forge links with the people, historically referred to as 'the democracy' and now known to political managers as 'the punters'. 'The Whigs' at the top of the political parties, she contends, will concede reform only if they are pushed.

Representatives in Parliament are not, in one sense at least, representative of their electorate. The Commons is made up predominantly of middle-class, white men. Anna Kruthoffer examines the links between the voting system and the under-representation of just over half the population. The Single Transferable Vote, she argues, would put more women in Parliament, enhance voter choice and avoid resort to quotas or other forms of special treatment.

Sarah Benton investigates the 'Curious Amnesia' of the English about their political history. The current fashion for 'charters', she contends, conceals a breakdown of the relationship between rulers and ruled, leading to a myriad of unrepresented communities and protest groups.

David Martin assesses the impact of the European Community on the reform question. Illustrating the role of proportionality in the construction of consensus, he draws parallels between the emerging politics of the Community and the political traditions and practices of Scotland.

Chris Game and Steve Leach look at another tier of the governance of Britain where single-party rule is no longer the norm. 'No overall control' has become an accepted part of political life in the hung councils. Tracing the ways local politicians have overcome fears of impending chaos, 'The Decline of the One Party State' draws out the positive benefits which 'NOC' has produced for the workings of local government, and examine its effects on the game-plans of local parties.

The complexities and sheer variety of questions considered in *Refreshing the Parts* demonstrate that electoral reform cannot be detached from wider aspects of British politics. Defenders of First-Past-the-Post rightly point out that a voting system reflects the idiosyncratic characteristics of a society and its historical development. The view of the MP as repesentative of a particular area, trudging through the wet winter's night to his 'advice surgery', is peculiarly British: members of the Bundesrag are legislators, not quasi-social workers. This view predates the emergence of modern party politics, but is none the weaker for that. The MORI 'State of the Nation' poll for the Joseph Rowntree Trust in 1991 found that around half of the population could correctly name their MP.

At the same time, electoral reform is bound up with the politics of Westminster, with what John Biffen called 'deals done to promote certain political interests'. To emulate Francis Place, as suggested by Nina Fishman in 'Whigs and Punters', reformers will have to steer change through an unreformed Commons. This will be far from easy, and there is no shining path which guarantees success. Despite the clear signs of movement reported in 'The Pattens, Plant and Paddy', no one should underestimate the strength of vested interest or the power of inertia.

I would like to thank the Joseph Rowntree Charitable Trust for their financial support. Those with whom I have discussed electoral reform over the past eight months are too numerous to acknowledge; but I should particularly like to thank John Biffen, Nina Fishman, Mary Georghiou, David Marquand, Helen Margetts, Austin Mitchell, Simon Osborn, Robin Squire, Robert Waller and Stuart Weir, all of whom have been very helpful, thought-provoking or both. In the preparation of the book, Peter Collins' dry humour was much appreciated, as was Stephen Robinson's eye for detail. Matt Seaton at Lawrence & Wishart remained unflappable. All contributors, of course, write in a personal capacity.

Gareth Smyth
February 1992

1

CLOSING THE WESTMINSTER CLUB

DAVID MARQUAND

Debate over proportional representation has been going on for more than a century, and the arguments for it are familiar. The simplest, and perhaps the most telling, is the argument *from justice*. If a party that gets a quarter of the popular vote wins only one-thirtieth of the members of parliament, not only it, but the people who voted for it, have been treated unjustly. If Labour voters in the south of England, or Conservative voters in the Labour heartlands of the north, are effectively denied parliamentary representation, they are unjustly discriminated against. No system can be perfectly fair, but the system we have now is so grotesquely unfair that it ought to be changed. Because that argument is so simple and so telling, it is the one we hear most frequently; and it is none the worse for that.

Closely linked to it is the argument *from democracy*. Since the principle of representative democracy first made its revolutionary appearance in the modern world, it has centred on the slogan – 'one person, one vote, one value'. First manhood suffrage and then adult suffrage, the secret ballot and equal electoral districts, were all mechanisms for making that slogan effective, and fierce battles had to be fought before they were achieved. But in this country, the victory was incomplete. The secret ballot and more or less equal electoral districts came in the nineteenth century. Adult suffrage came in the 1920s. But although the principle of one person, one vote was satisfied, the principle of one vote, one value was not. Votes given to what the Westminster establishment patronisingly refers to as minor parties are manifestly less valuable than votes given to the big parties. And because of that, our democracy is flawed.

The argument from democracy is not heard quite as often as the argument from justice, but it too is pretty common – and rightly so. There is also a third argument, however, and because it is less familiar than the other two I want to concentrate on it. It is not easy to define in a single phrase. It has to do with the curious way in which democracy came to this country, with the nature of our political establishment and with the relationship between that establishment and the people for whom it claims to speak.

We like to think that the British Parliament is the mother of parliaments, and Britain the cradle of democracy. There is something in the first point, but the second is a myth. We had parliamentary government at an early stage in our history, but we did not become a democracy until well within living memory. Women did not get the vote until after the first world war. Nor did large numbers of working-class men. In 1914, Imperial Germany had a more democratic suffrage in national elections than we did. (To be fair, it was much less democratic in other ways.) And democracy came to us in dribs and drabs, as a gift from the magic circle of Westminster politicians, neither through a popular uprising, nor a comprehensive reconstruction of the old, pre-democratic constitution which had gradually evolved through generations of custom.

In some ways, this was a blessing. The spectre of civil war disappeared from mainland Britain with the defeat of the Jacobite rising of 1745. We escaped the savage political conflicts, the bloodshed and butchery, that so often ravaged our continental neighbours: there was never a guillotine in Trafalgar Square; we knew no Red Terror or White counter-Terror. But, as so often in life, the blessing had a price tag. The relationship between the political establishment and the people never really changed. Over time new men, and even the occasional new woman, were admitted to the establishment; through them, new groups won a place in the political sun and new influences were brought to bear on the making of public policy. But the establishment remained the establishment. Its new members took on the assumptions of the old ones. They changed it, of course; but *it changed them* far more. Radical businessmen, Liberal professionals, working-class Labour leaders in turn won admission to the 'Westminster Club'. But it was still a club, and our system was still permeated with its pre-democratic values and presuppositions. Governments governed, leaders led and followers knew their place.

It will take more than a change in the electoral system to break down the club walls. But although proportional representation will not do the trick all by itself, it is a precondition of the wider and deeper changes that are needed to create a truly civic culture in this country. For the existing electoral system has created a kind of political duopoly. The two big parties run the club between them; and they take it in turns to control the huge engine of power centred upon it. So long as the duopoly lasts – so long as each duopolist knows that, if the cards fall its way, it will have total control of the engine of power – both will remain enmeshed in the assumptions of club government. And that is another way of saying that both will continue to view the public outside the walls as the raw material for top-down social engineering rather than as active citizens making their own history from the bottom up.

In the end, then, this argument too is a fairly simple one. Monopoly is bad, not just for the customer, but for the monopolist. The same applies to duopoly. It is not only the voters who suffer: in a thousand subtle ways, the duopolists suffer as well. After all, they too are part of the culture. And the culture of duopoly is a culture of manipulation – a culture in which, to use Vaclav Havel's resounding phrase, it becomes progressively more difficult to 'live in truth'. No system is proof against the corruption of power, but some systems encourage it more than others. In our system, it is part of the air which political leaders breathe. Change is overdue.

2
QUOTE ... UNQUOTE

Compiled by PETER HANINGTON

'I have just been handed a hot political potato.'
Professor Raymond Plant, *The Times*, 30 October 1990

'The British people cannot get a stable government, nor a government representing a majority of the electors, nor in the long run the efficient and faithful conduct of their affairs ... We are no longer entitled to look down upon continental parliaments.'
Winston Churchill, *Sunday Chronicle*, 2 March 1924

'There is a wind of change stirring in Labour's grassroots. This is the voice of the constituencies where the Tories got their majority in three general elections.'
Robin Cook, *Guardian*, 27 May 1991

'PR increases the number of parties and hence the chances of an indecisive result. The coalitions would be cobbled together after the election. The electorate voting for a horse would get a camel.'
Michael Meacher, *Daily Telegraph*, 13 May 1991

'[PR] does leave minority parties determining government policy, and striking bargains for their support. That is not democracy, that is horse trading and I will have no part of it.'
John Major, *Independent*, 8 May 1991

'English people fancy they are free: it is only during the election of members of parliament that they are so.'
Jean Jacques Rousseau, *The Social Contract*, 1762

'We are certainly not going to play Meccano sets with the British constitution in order to secure an illusory gain in circumstances which are not going to exist.'
Chris Patten, *Independent*, 31 July 1991

'It is no longer a question of whether Labour will commit itself to electoral reform but when, and for what elections.'
Robin Cook, *Financial Times*, 13 July 1991

'Since PR will deprive at least a third of all existing MPs of their seats, one might as well ask turkeys to vote for Christmas. The Alternative Vote is the only scheme a majority of MPs might back. Politically, both STV and the Additional Member System are complete non-starters.'
Professor Ivor Crewe, *Marxism Today*, October 1991

'They thought they could improve on the British system by introducing an elaborate form of proportional representation. The result was the splitting up of parties and the multiplication of small groups ... The failure to produce effective leadership was one of the chief arguments used by Hitler to discredit parliamentary democracy.'
Professor Agnes Headlam-Morley, *The Times* (letters), 11 June 1975

'If you like government by coalition, then vote for PR. It might seem more democratic to have raving loonies and greens in Parliament, but it is doubtful if it would lead to better Government.'
Lord Dunalley, *Daily Telegraph* (letters), 16 May 1991

'The Party will not in the end support an electoral system that prevents Labour from ever again governing in its own right.'
Roy Hattersley, Labour Party conference, Blackpool, 1990

'All these years we have confused real strength of government with the mere ability of a single party to command a majority in the House of Commons. Real strength lies in the ability to interpret the true wishes of the people and to find compromises between their conflicting interests.'
Anthony Wigram, *Observer* (letters), 3 November 1973

'The only hope of resuscitation for the CPGB (Communist Party) lies in a system of proportional representation loose enough to let a few from its ranks through the net ... I trust that no other party will be silly

enough to swallow the bait of a manoeuvre the only purpose of which is
to get a CP member elected to Parliament.'
Bernard Levin, *The Times*, 15 July 1991

'People who are entirely defensive about the possibility of change are
simply not in touch with the fact that people's opinions in the country
are much more dynamic and forward-looking than some politicians give
them credit for.'
Neil Kinnock, *The World This Weekend*, BBC Radio 4, 5 January 1992

'A democratic electoral system should reflect as fairly as possible the
wishes of voters. It must also protect the majority of voters from
flagrant minority rule. British elections have begun to fail on both
counts.'
Adam Raphael, *The Observer*, 1983

'Unprompted, Prince Charles has talked himself into a constitutional
quagmire ... here is the heritage-cherishing prince, who would go to the
block to preserve an oriel window or champion the Cranmer Prayer
Book, now wishing on us a functional voting system utterly out of
keeping with our democratic traditions. Next time HRH feels unable to
keep to himself his view on PR, he would be better advised to tell it to
the trees.'
Daily Mail (leader), 7 March 1991

'Our existing Constitution can be likened to an ancient house ... The
reformers look on this extraordinary structure with disdain and pro-
nounce it fit only for demolition. In their arrogance and simple-
mindedness, they resemble the architects and planners who thought that
by knocking down old town centres, and erecting modern, rational
structures in their place, a great leap forward in human happiness could
be made.'
Andrew Gimson, *Spectator*, 2 November 1991

'Electoral reform is the most important change we can make that is
compatible with the history of our institutions and with our political
philosophy.'
Chris Patten, *The Tory Case*, 1983

'In a sense the outcomes of politics are not legitimate unless the
procedures are seen to be legitimate as well. And I think there is a sense

6

in which the procedures are beginning to be seen as illegitimate.'
Professor Raymond Plant, *Independent*, 4 November 1991

'Putting Roy Hattersley in charge of constitutional reform was as sensible as bringing back Stalin to handle perestroika.'
Austin Mitchell, *Guardian*, 2 April 1991

'PR does not produce more checks on the executive; it produces the kind of shabby, corrupt compromises now current in the Anglican Church, which, of course, has become Noddyland in gloria excelsis.'
Henry Hobhouse, *Daily Telegraph* (letters), 17 July 1991

'Recognising the need for fair votes means ensuring the reality of a truly representative Parliament. And that, in all likelihood, means the fact of coalition governments ... None of us enter elections seeking to share power - but if such a question arises during the campaign itself then all parties must be prepared to address it constructively. We will. So must Labour.'
Charles Kennedy, Liberal Democrat Spring conference, Nottingham, 1991

'The average lifetime of an Italian government is the gestation period of a horse.'
The Economist (leader), 20 April 1991

'Had the (German) elections been held on the British or American systems, the Nazi Party would have won every seat in the Reichstag.'
Hermann Goering, Nuremburg, 13 March 1946

'No government which is in a large minority, even if it possesses a working majority in the House of Commons, can have the necessary power to cope with real problems.'
Winston Churchill, *Sunday Chronicle*, 2 March 1924

'... the proportional representation of all opinions and interests by means of the single transferable vote with constituencies returning at least five members.'
Resolution adopted by Trades Union Congress, 1922

'Life isn't fair, you cannot produce a fair voting system.'
Dennis Skinner, Labour Party conference, October 1991

'You get middle-class articulate groups around Charter 88, but show me a public gathering in Oswestry who will have foregathered to denounce the present electoral system as they would foregather to denounce the inequities of the community charge.'
John Biffen, *Marxism Today*, October 1991

'The English electoral system is nothing but an open fraud. In a dozen ways it is gerrymandered in the interests of the moneyed classes ... a foreign observer sees only the huge inequality of wealth, the unfair electoral system ... and concludes that democracy is simply a polite name for dictatorship.'
George Orwell, 'Socialism and the English Genius', in *The Lion and the Unicorn*, 1941

'It is important that we close the gap that now exists between the number of votes that a party gets and the number of seats it gathers. I think in a small country, in Scotland, if you're starting with a clean sheet - and we have that advantage - then I think that distortion is one that is now no longer possible to defend.'
Donald Dewar, *Glasgow Herald*, 10 December 1991

'Once PR was accepted for any major elections in mainland Britain the pressure to extend it to all elections would become irresistible.'
The Proportional Pantomime, briefing sponsored by seventeen Labour Euro-MPs, 1990

'Parliament has joined the monarchy as a dignified, not an effective, element in the constitution.'
Richard Crossman, *Diary*, 1959

'PR is as easy as 1,2,3.'
Government-sponsored booklet for the 1973 Northern Ireland district council elections

3

THE PATTENS, PLANT AND PADDY: WHERE THE PARTIES STAND

GARETH SMYTH

Conservative MP Robin Squire has compared politicians' support for electoral reform with a see-saw: 'As it increases in one of the parties, it reduces in the other. It's very difficult to get both ends of the see-saw up at the same time.'[1] Much past evidence supports his view.

Historically, Labour's interest in reform diminished after 1918 once it overtook the Liberals and became challenger in a two-party system. The Liberals had many opportunities before 1914 to reform the voting system, but it was only when relegated to the status of a third party that they became wholehearted champions of proportional representation. As a party of government for the whole of the modern era, the Conservatives have with good reason regarded themselves as beneficiaries of First-Past-the-Post.

Since the hung parliament of 1974, the 'Squire see-saw' has been going up and down. Conservative interest in electoral reform was greatest when in opposition between 1974 and 1979, and diminished in office. Labour interest has grown gradually over the eleven years in opposition from Mrs Thatcher's first victory in 1979 to the establishment of the Plant committee in 1990.

At the same time, however, a number of wider factors have brought electoral reform up the political agenda. European integration, the growth of support for smaller parties, and the increased number of 'safe' seats, have created a different framework in which calculations about party advantage are made. While it is true that, in John Biffen's words, electoral reform would need to result from 'certain deals done to promote certain political interests',[2] there is now a momentum behind change not present in the 1950s, 1960s or even 1970s.

THE PATTENS

In July 1991, four days before Professor Raymond Plant launched the interim report of Labour's working party on electoral reform, the broadsheet papers reported a speech by Home Office minister John Patten. In the first major constitutional pronouncement by a member of John Major's government, Mr Patten informed a Conservative Political Centre summer school that PR 'delivers a government and a spatchcocked programme that no one could ever have voted for'. Here, ready made, was the Tory thumbs-down to Plant.

But Conservative commitment to First-Past-the-Post has not been unwavering, and is far from even. In 1973 Edward Heath's Conservative Government introduced the single transferable vote in Northern Ireland for Assembly and district council elections, a method of voting extended by Labour in 1979 to European elections in the province. When Heath lost his Commons majority in the infamous 'who runs the country?' election on 28 February 1974, he unsuccessfully attempted over the weekend of 1-4 March to reach an agreement with Liberal leader Jeremy Thorpe: Heath offered a speaker's conference on electoral reform, which proved an insufficiently tempting carrot for the Liberals. Having fallen from power to be replaced by a minority Labour administration, Heath advocated the creation of a cross-party government in the election of October 1974.

When Labour won a parliamentary majority in October 1974 with less than 40 per cent of the popular vote, many Tories looked seriously at possibilities for electoral reform. There was a genuine sense in Tory ranks that Britain was becoming ungovernable, stemming largely from the role of the trade unions in defeating pay policy. Quaint as it now seems, many feared the Wilson Government would carry out manifesto commitments of increased nationalisation and 'a fundamental and irreversible shift in the balance of wealth and power in favour of working people and their families'.

Sir Ian Gilmour wrote in 1977 that 'electoral reform would help to deal not only with the first threat to the constitution of social forces refusing to obey Parliament but also with the second threat of an extremist Labour Party imposing Marxist chains upon an unwilling country.'[3] Nicholas Scott, later a junior minister under Margaret Thatcher and John Major, suggested that 'at a time when the democratic process is under more threat than at any time since the end of the war, we should be at pains to see that it is fair, relevant and as defensible as we can make it.'[4] From the shadow cabinet, Francis Pym told the 1977 Tory Conference that 'it would be most unwise for the Party to close its mind to the possibilities that could be opened up by electoral change'.[5]

The Party's backers were as interested as its MPs. A 1975 pamphlet from Aims for Freedom and Enterprise illustrated growing sympathy among businesses, and Norman Lamont expressed the fear that 'too much talk of electoral reform has caused some misguided industrialists to withhold financial support from the Conservative Party.' In January 1977 the *Sun* published a Marplan poll registering popular desire for change. In a 1977 Commons debate, Neil Kinnock mocked the Liberals for seeking to revive their 'dwindling coffers' through support for PR, and funding was also attracted by Conservative Action for Electoral Reform (CAER).

But the Conservative reformers were defeated in conference debates in 1975 and 1978. New Tory leader Margaret Thatcher set a radical course eschewing compromise, and won three elections with under 44 per cent of the vote. Tory interest in electoral reform waned, and although CAER continued to organise annual fringe meetings at Party conference it gave up its full-time office in the early 1980s. The reformers were biding their time.

Tim Rathbone MP carried out a survey of Conservative MPs just before the 1983 election. He still carries the figures in his wallet: 123 were either 'in favour of or prepared to think about' a reformed system for the Commons, and 116 against. While Rathbone's survey illustrated the flexibility on which British Conservatism generally prides itself, it is notable that no one has carried out a survey since. Under the leadership of Margaret Thatcher, electoral reform was not perceived as a pressing matter.

Following the advent of John Major, the Tory wets emerged, blinking, into the daylight. Most Tory electoral reformers are on the wet wing of the Party, and with Labour's Plant commission attracting attention they began to turn their minds to what had been regarded as a 'non-issue' for several years.

John Major chose Chris Patten as Conservative Party chairman. Patten had reportedly been a member of CAER and had advocated electoral reform in *The Tory Case*, published in 1983. In June 1991 Patten announced on the TV programme *The Pursuit of Power* that 'the case for electoral reform ... is less markedly an important feature of the agenda in the late eighties or early nineties': this was, in Mr Patten's view, because after eleven years of Mrs Thatcher, government was both 'respectable and possible again'.

Nevertheless, Chris Patten chose as his parliamentary private secretary the Hornchurch MP and vice-President of the Electoral Reform Society, Robin Squire, whose enthusiasm for electoral reform remained undiminished. In an interview in June 1991, Squire acknowledged the extent of opposition among Tory MPs:

> My impression is that most of the '83 and '87 intakes, a very large proportion, are not supporters. That may reflect being selected in the shadow of Margaret, and her uncompromising opposition. A number of Conservatives will concede that the present system is unfair, but they will nonetheless shy away from reform on the basis that it would be the end of strong government.[6]

At the same time, Robin Squire felt that in a hung Parliament 'Party leaders would not reject discussions, but my guess is that they would ultimately flounder unless there were a subsequent election which was also inconclusive.' Former cabinet minister John Biffen was pursuing a similar line of thought, suggesting in a slightly mischievous *Guardian* article in July 1991 that Conservatives would have to 'mark their cards on electoral reform' in the event of a hung Parliament. Biffen floated the tantalising possibility of a Conservative/Labour deal to 'dish the Whigs' by introducing the Alternative Vote.

Biffen elaborated his pragmatism in *Marxism Today*, criticising Chris Patten for an 'ideological' approach to the issue. He went on:

> If I were trying to start again in politics and see through the murk into the future, I would keep my powder dry as far as the constitutional reforms were concerned, because by being too intransigent I could drive together Labour and Liberal. I'm in business on a division between Labour and Liberal.[7]

While John Biffen contemplated the goings-on of smoke-filled rooms, Conservative Action for Electoral Reform was spluttering back into life. In typical Tory fashion, CAER has always been much less

THE SUN, Monday, January 31, 1977   9

THE BIG ISSUES ARE ALWAYS BIGGEST IN THE SUN

Let the people rule!

By Roger Carroll
POLITICAL EDITOR

SEVEN OUT OF TEN WANT A FAIRER VOTING SYSTEM

BRITAIN is in the mood for a revolution. A peaceful one.

Popular demands for a drastic change echo thunderously through an exclusive Sun poll today on the way we are ruled.

The special survey, carried out by top pollsters Marplan, reveals beyond a doubt that people are fed up and furious with the present political system.

And a strong tide of opinion is flowing above all for a new and fairer method of picking our MPs.

Next priorities in the popular revolution are more referendums, and fixed-term Parliaments.

The general feeling is that the system no longer delivers the goods.

Disillusion is deepest with the political parties themselves, and their inability to rescue the nation from crisis.

Almost two adults in every three — 65 per cent—do not believe that any party can solve either the economic or political problems facing Britain.

Contempt

Only 37 per cent still have faith in our politicians to do the trick.

The young are by far the most disillusioned.

Of the under-35s, 68 per cent say the politicians are incapable, compared with 58 per cent of the over-65s.

As individuals, local MPs are held in contempt.

Only about one person in seven (15 per cent) believe his local MP has done much for his constituency.

And as few as one in 14 (seven per cent) think he has done a lot in Parliament to help solve Britain's problems.

Once again, the young are the most scornful. Only two per cent of the under-35s reckon their MP has done "a lot" in Parliament.

So how can we stop the rot?

Marplan put five ideas for reform to the electors: a proportional voting system, referendums, a shake-up of the House of Lords, fixed-term Parliaments, and devolution.

Q Which system would be most fair to British voters?

PERCENTAGES	ALL	CON	LAB	LIB
Proportional representation	75	76	66	81
Existing system	50	58	44	9

Q Which of these two results would you have preferred at the last election?

PERCENTAGES	ALL	CON	LAB	LIB
Proportional representation	79	74	66	94
Existing system	36	58	51	6

Q How well does Parliament represent your personal interests and concerns?

PERCENTAGES	ALL	MEN	WOMEN
Not at all well / not very well	73	73	73
Very well / quite well	57	57	57

Q How capable is any political party of solving the problems facing Britain?

PERCENTAGES	ALL ADULTS	AGED 18-34	AGED 29-64	AGED 65+
Not very / not at all capable	65	64	63	58
Very / quite capable	37	35	37	43

Q Should Britain have:

PERCENTAGES	ALL	CON	LAB	LIB
Frequent referendums?	53	54	53	53
Occasional referendums?	47	46	47	48
No more referendums?	51	39	54	38

Q Is the existing House of Lords a good or bad thing for Britain?

PERCENTAGES	ALL	CON	LAB	LIB
Very or quite good	76	44	49	60
Very or quite bad	36	18	31	31

Q Which of these would you prefer?

PERCENTAGES	ALL	CON	LAB	LIB
Leave the House of Lords as it is	58	65	43	60
Replace the House of Lords by a second elected House	18	25	18	24
Abolish House of Lords	10	7	19	10

Q Which of these is the most important in improving how Britain is governed?

PERCENTAGES	ALL	CON	LAB	LIB
New system of electing MPs	34	30	38	43
Fixed Term Elections	18	17	18	19
More referendums	18	18	18	18
Reform of House of Lords	8	13	7	9
Scottish & Welsh Devolution	5	5	5	5
Devolution of English Regions	2	2	2	1
None of these	13	15	13	6

'Politicians can't deliver the goods'

They described the changes that would have made on the outcome of the October, 1974, General Election.

More than seven out of ten adults replied that the proportional system would be fairer to the voters.

A mere 28 per cent reckoned the old system was fairer.

Three Tories out of every four admitted that proportional representation (PR) was fairer.

Even Labour voters, whose side gained most from the old method, agreed, by 36 per cent to 44.

The Liberals, not surprisingly, also supported by a thumping majority of ten to one.

Asked next if they would have preferred the election result announced by PR, people

Support

REFERENDUMS

HOUSE OF LORDS:

Left Wing losers

NO ONE loves the Left. Except, perhaps, Mrs Margaret Thatcher.

Because they are driving thousands of Labour voters into her arms.

This is shown clearly in Marplan's study of the influence a Left or Right-wing Labour candidate has on his party's chances.

The more Left-wing the candidate, the bigger the swing to the Tories.

And especially among trade unionists.

Britain's current voting intentions, claims Marplan, give the Tories a 16 per cent lead.

But the picture changes when people are asked: "How would you vote if your local Labour candidate strongly supported the views of people like Roy Jenkins, Reg Prentice and Shirley Williams?"

The result then is sharp drop in the Tory lead, from 16 to 1 points.

And among trade unionists Labour turns an eight per cent deficit into an eight per cent lead.

No dictator here

WOULD-BE Napoleons can forget it. In spite of our grumbles people do not want a dictator in Britain.

Only one person in ten reckons that a strong regime which would rule without elections is what we need.

More than one in five of the under-35s (23 per cent) would prefer a government that ruled without elections.

Enoch Powell emerges as favourite to be dictator—if we were to have one. He is backed by 31 per cent.

Next comes ex-Tory Premier Edward Heath (16 per cent), and the Queen (16 per cent).

Nearly three out of every four (72 per cent) feel that Parliament does not properly deal with the things they most care about.

But trade unions, not politicians, get most blame for our troubles.

WHAT DO YOU THINK? WRITE TO THE SUN
Send your views to: Politics, The Sun, 30 Bouverie St., London EC4Y 8DE

The Sun, 31 January 1977. © *The Sun*/Rex Features, 1977. Reproduced by kind permission.

vociferous than its opposite number, the Labour Campaign for Electoral Reform. Its work has centred around the parliamentary Party rather than constituency associations. At the Blackpool Conference in October 1991, motions on electoral reform found insufficient support to be debated, although CAER did hold a small fringe meeting.

Of leading Conservatives, Douglas Hurd, Chris Patten, Lynda Chalker and Tim Renton have all been members of CAER: Kenneth Baker, Nicholas Scott, Peter Brooke and Malcolm Rifkind have backed PR either for European elections or Scottish/Welsh assemblies. Backbench supporters include Julian Critchley, David Knox and Gerry Neale. Among sixty-one Conservative MPs who voted in 1977 for proportional representation for European Parliament elections were Hugh Dykes, Edward Heath, Tony Newton, Timothy Raison and Sir George Young.

Both Robin Squire and John Biffen have insisted that the Party would not attempt a whip on a constitutional issue. In any Commons vote to reform the electoral system, the Tory reformers would be crucial.

PLANT

Labour's love affair with First-Past-the-Post, perhaps surprisingly, survived the demise of the Callaghan Government in the accumulated rubbish and unburied bodies of the 'winter of discontent'. Many in Labour's ranks believed that greater accountability to activists would rescue the Party from declining popularity, and the 'Bennite left' initially swept all before it. By 1981 the Party conference supported unilateral nuclear disarmament, abolition of the Lords, withdrawal from the EEC and massive public spending increases.

Internal constitutional preoccupations and the swing to the left led to the departure of the 'Gang of Four' to form the SDP. Thirty-two Labour MPs (and one Conservative) switched. Labour went on to fight the 1983 election on a manifesto dubbed 'the longest suicide note in history'. Not even the scale of Labour's defeat – 15 per cent behind the Conservatives and only 2 per cent ahead of the SDP/Liberal Alliance – led to a serious examination of electoral reform. The Party turned instead to a new leader, Neil Kinnock, offering youth and energy, and to a new public relations supremo, Peter Mandelson, offering professionalism and roses.

Despite good local election results in May 1986, the autumn saw the demise of Labour's poll lead, and with the looming possibility of a third successive general election defeat, in early 1987 some in Labour's ranks broke cover. Stuart Weir, editor of the *New Socialist*, published articles examining electoral reform and anti-Tory tactical voting, only to discover that Labour's belief in editorial independence and a free press did not extend to its own magazine – Weir was sacked.

The third Thatcher government was crucial in shifting perceptions. Although Labour had run an impressive 1987 election campaign (epitomised by Hugh Hudson's 'Kinnock: the Movie'), it was still 11.5 per cent behind the victorious Mrs Thatcher, who found herself with a majority of 101 seats on a little over 42 per cent of the vote. The subsequent imposition of the poll tax on a reluctant Parliament and an even more reluctant country weakened Labour's belief in the First-Past-the-Post system which, in Robin Cook's words, 'made Thatcher possible and sustained her so long in office'.[8]

Another important factor was geographical polarisation. The picture of a 'blue' south and a 'red' north was extremely simplified, but the rise of the Liberals and shrinkage of the number of marginal seats under First-Past-the-Post produced huge swathes of southern England where Labour could not break through: in 1987 the Party won 1.7 million votes (350,000 more than in Scotland) outside London south of a line from the Wash to the Severn, but only three seats. To the dismay of party managers, voters in these southern seats began to regard a Labour vote as 'wasted'.

The Labour Campaign for Electoral Reform (LCER) now grew steadily. In 1988 it gained an important asset in Jeff Rooker, the assiduous MP for Birmingham Perry Barr, who as chairman set it the task of working patiently to win votes through the constituency parties and trade unions. Austin Mitchell, the pro-reform MP for Great Grimsby, later remarked that 'Rooker was the turning point. We'd been a bit academic before, but he convinced us it's no good giving lectures, we'd got to go out and convince people it's in their interests.'[9] LCER took on a part-time officer, the persuasive and persistent Mary Georghiou, and, following a tactic pioneered by the Bennite Campaign for Labour Party Democracy, circulated model resolutions to constituency parties and trade unions. Georghiou also took on the task of wooing MPs.

It was hard work, but it was to prove crucial. LCER fought an astute campaign – its very use of the term 'electoral reform' reflecting an unwillingness to back any particular system or to encourage fundamentalism. With the lucid Scot Robin Cook arguing for reform from within the shadow cabinet, LCER was becoming a formidable team.

When Labour embarked on its policy review in the autumn of 1987, the electoral system was not up for discussion. The 'final report' of the review, *Meet the Challenge, Make the Change*, published in 1989, merely noted that a proposed new second chamber might be elected by a different method to the Commons. A shortened up-date, *Looking to the Future*, published May 1990, expressly stated that 'Labour is opposed to changing the electoral system for the Commons'.

But LCER was chipping away at the monolith. Conference resolutions and amendments supporting electoral reform increased from twenty-five in 1987 to thirty-seven in 1989 when a pro-PR motion was comfortably defeated. In Dunoon in March 1990 came the first clear triumph, when Labour's Scottish Conference voted against First-Past-the-Post for the proposed Scottish Assembly. The decision was born partly of a desire to create national consensus across the Scottish Constitutional Convention and partly from the belief that the 1978 devolution referendum had failed through voters' fear of a Parliament dominated by the Labour Party and the central belt (by 'Glasgow councillors and Edinburgh lawyers', as George Galloway put it). But Dunoon provided a vital new addition to the reformers' arsenal: Labour in Scotland were accepting electoral reform from a position of strength, not as an admission of weakness.

In October 1990 came the crucial breakthrough: against the advice of Labour's national executive, and with LCER lobbying furiously behind the scenes, delegates voted to include the House of Commons within the remit of a working party originally intended to review electoral systems for the second chamber and the Scottish Assembly. Ron Todd, leader of the Transport Workers, whose votes tipped the balance, was taken aback by the amount of press interest and exclaimed to delegates 'Goodness me, comrades, what a fuss!'

Suddenly it was eminently respectable within Labour's ranks to advocate proportional representation. The working party under Raymond Plant, the bearded politics professor from Southampton University, went quietly about its task. *Opportunity Britain*, launched in May 1991, coyly noted that 'it may be that different electoral systems may be appropriate for different institutions', so keeping everyone on board.

But the reformers were winning the argument and things moved quickly. The Electoral Reform Society's (ERS) campaign manager since June 1989, Simon Osborn, had been playing an increasing behind-the-scenes role in Labour's shift, both in lobbying trade unions and in judicious press briefings. Osborn now commissioned a MORI poll asking voters who they would vote for if Labour backed PR. The results, published in April 1991, dangled tempting prizes before the Labour leadership: the Party could pick up one in five Liberal Democrat supporters by backing PR, achieving a 4.5 per cent swing from the Conservatives in London and the south and a 2 per cent swing in the Midlands, areas containing fifty-five of the ninety-seven seats Labour needed for an overall majority.

When the BBC's *Today* programme broadcast these findings, the ERS were contacted by Labour's Walworth Road HQ. It was only once the details of the poll were faxed through that an election team orchestrated by Peter Mandelson allowed Labour candidate Huw Edwards to proclaim his faith in electoral reform on the Friday afternoon before polling in the crucial Monmouth by-election. The tactic was itself opportunistic, but Edwards' views were not atypical of the new crop of Labour hopefuls: a poll of 102 Labour candidates in Tory-held marginals revealed that fifty-nine backed a change of voting system and that only nine wanted to keep First-Past-the-Post.

In July the interim report of the Plant committee leaned towards PR at least for bodies other than the Commons. The 40,000-word *Democracy, Representation and Elections* was instantly dubbed 'The Plant Report'. Its publication attracted much media interest, and the *Guardian* sold copies at £7.95 to the general public. The report – a weighty, often technical, and generally hedged analysis – was written largely by Professor Plant. It made a crucial distinction between 'legislative' bodies and 'deliberative' bodies. For 'deliberative' bodies, such as the European Parliament and an elected second chamber, the report was sympathetic towards PR. For 'legislative' bodies, meaning principally the Commons, the report expressly ruled out STV and emphasised the importance of retaining a constituency link and of allowing voters a clear choice of government. The argument was compatible with the retention of First-Past-the-Post for the Commons, or with a switch to the Alternative Vote or even AMS. Different systems, the report clearly suggested, could be appropriate for different institutions. Neil Kinnock said the report provided the basis for 'open and informed debate', and Party managers were keen to point out that it was the most substantial tome on the subject ever

Nicholas Garland, *The Independent*, 29 September 1989. © Nicholas Garland, 1989. Reproduced by kind permission.

produced by a British political party. Deputy leader Roy Hatt
welcomed the report while gently restating his commitmen
First-Past-the-Post for elections to the Commons.

But the argument for the *status quo* was increasingly in the hand
the hard left and was sounding increasingly creaky. The First Past
Post (FPTP) Campaign was initiated on 30 January 1991 by Campai
Group MP Bob Cryer, and supported by the Campaign for Labo
Party Democracy which had led the opposition to one-memb
one-vote within the Party itself. The FPTP Campaign's basic case wa
that PR would prevent Labour ever again winning a majority on it
own: 'It is correct to consider PR from the angle of its effect on Labour
because Labour represents the defence of ordinary people in this
country.'[10] Other arguments tended to reflect the style and contents of
the late 1970s and early 1980s when the Labour left had talked to a
dwindling band of the faithful.

Dennis Skinner told a FPTP fringe at the Brighton conference 1991
that 'you can't have PR on the picket line.' At a fringe meeting at the
local government conference in a snow-bound Nottingham in
February, an FPTP campaign founder-member denounced a
questioner as 'middle-class' for daring to suggest that the debate was
about good government and fair representation rather than Labour's
interests.

Apart from Roy Hattersley, leading figures believed to favour the
status quo were keeping their heads down. The rearguard action of the
Campaign for Electoral Success in Scotland, formed as late as February
1991, was led by a front-bencher, foreign affairs spokesman George
Foulkes, but not a single member of the shadow cabinet spoke at the
FPTP fringe rally at the Brighton conference in October 1991. Both
Bryan Gould and Jack Cunningham were reported to be sympathetic
to change. By the end of 1991 the FPTP Campaign had to admit in its
first annual report to a 'depressingly small number of members': only
fifteen MPs, seven Euro-MPs and thirty-seven ordinary Party
members had signed up.

The official pro-Plant line was carried at Brighton in October 1991
by 3,533,000 votes to 980,000, the majority increased by 2,344,000 in
just a year. The confidence of the reformers was evident in their use of
the 'c' word: Jeff Rooker told the LCER fringe, 'It's the voters'
decision and we are duty bound to accept it … That's not defeatism,
that's not an argument for coalition, that's not an argument for deals
behind closed doors, that's an argument for a democratic process.'

In Scotland the pace was picking up even more. On 15 November the executive of the Scottish Constitutional Convention (the body set up by Labour and Liberal politicians, the churches, local authorities and small businesses to draw up proposals for a Scottish Assembly) agreed the broad outlines of a PR voting system for a Scottish Assembly. As options coalesced around variations of the Additional Member System, George Foulkes told *Scotland on Sunday* in December – 'I would prefer to stick to First-Past-the-Post, but if others are prepared to compromise then so am I.'[11]

The Scottish Constitutional Convention was attracting admirers south of Hadrian's Wall. In November, an emboldened Professor Plant suggested that First-Past-the-Post was 'beginning to be seen as illegitimate': dismissing talk of any post-election deal between political parties to achieve electoral reform, Plant instead floated the idea of a 'constitutional convention', which he described as 'entirely a personal one of mine'. By an unlikely coincidence, LCER chairman Jeff Rooker had told a meeting in Cambridge five days earlier, 'We need nothing less than an electoral convention, a new body to look at a new democracy for all our people.'

All this was consistent with the rhetoric being employed by the Labour leader. Determined even then not to be accused of panic or opportunism, Kinnock told a news conference in May 1991 that he realised 'two years ago that it is a very important debate'. In his keynote speech at Brighton Kinnock said electoral reform 'must be addressed with the fullest and widest public information, that is how we'll approach it in government'. On 5 January 1992 he told the BBC's *World this Weekend* audience he would not accept discussions on electoral reform 'as part of some trading' in a hung parliament. 'The British people are interested,' Kinnock continued, 'but the British people want more than anything else that kind of [rational] presentation and that kind of discussion so that they can make up their own minds.' The *Independent* led their front page the next day with the bold headline – 'Kinnock offers vote on electoral reform.'

PADDY

Liberal fortunes improved very slowly through the 1950s and 1960s. February 1974 brought the Liberals over six million votes and a 'hung' Parliament. Edward Heath invited Liberal leader Jeremy Thorpe for talks, in which Heath offered a royal commission on electoral reform.

The parliamentary Liberal party – concentrated on the 'celtic fringe' of Scotland, Wales and the west country – were emerging from a period of being the also-rans of British politics. Although it was not until the Monday 4 March that Heath resigned and the Queen sent for Harold Wilson, the negotiations had frightened politicians who had no real experience of exercising power.

When David Steel replaced Thorpe in 1976 he was determined that the Liberals would be be a party of government, not a party of protest. His first conference speech as leader, at Llandudno in 1976, outlined the need for coalition: the purists, including the Young Liberals, protested but Steel won the day. With Labour's tiny overall majority disappearing in by-election defeats, his opportunity arrived very quickly. The Lib-Lab pact of 1977-78 was important to Steel not so much because of any great concessions extracted, but because the mechanisms of consultation put the Liberals in the corridors of power. Steel also knew that his hand was weak: the Liberals had only thirteen MPs and as much to fear from an early election as Jim Callaghan.

When the SDP formed in 1981, Steel quickly saw the advantages of welcoming on board former cabinet ministers Roy Jenkins, Shirley Williams, David Owen and Bill Rodgers. In 1983 the Liberal/SDP Alliance polled only 675,985 votes fewer than Labour. But in 1987, after a lacklustre campaign, they fell further behind and the election of only twenty-two MPs was followed by a bout of political kami-kazi. Battles within both parts of the Alliance led to a merged party, the Social and Liberal Democrats, while a rump SDP led by David Owen headed surely, but slowly, into oblivion.

More was to come. The newly-merged party went through a series of disastrous wrangles about its name – the SLD, the Democrats, before settling on the Liberal Democrats – which saw a decline to a pitiful 6.2 per cent share of the vote in the European election of 1989, and was to remain in single figures in the polls until the autumn of 1990. Paddy Ashdown, elected to replace Steel in 1988, had a traumatic beginning as leader: the mould of two-party politics began to look stronger. But Ashdown's nerve held. At the beginning of 1991 he launched a new policy document, *Shaping Tomorrow: Starting Today*, which sought to project a distinct programme for a party in danger of being sandwiched by the centre-ground encroachment of Kinnock's new model Labour Party and Major's Conservatives. The Liberal Democrats bravely committed themselves to raising an extra penny from income tax should it prove necessary to 'improve the quality of education'. Ashdown grasped the nettle of European federalism in asserting 'the European Parliament must be given full powers of co-decision with the Council.'

Proportional representation remained an article of faith for Paddy's army, but Ashdown quickly instilled a hard professionalism. Blessed with charisma and the personable manner with Party activists which David Steel had often lacked, Paddy Ashdown found little opposition within the Party. The refusal of some fundamentalists to join a merged party eased a perceptible transition. *Guardian* columnist Ian Aitken quipped that, dressed in corduroys and sports coat, he was now the scruffiest person at Liberal conference. Following the inclusion of the Commons in the remit of Labour's Plant committee and with continuing negotiations in the Convention in Scotland, there was much in early 1991 to suggest that Labour was edging closer to the Liberal Democrats on the constitutional agenda – an agenda which was, after all, identified by the Liberal Democrats as 'the key to success in other areas of government responsibility' (*Changing Britain for Good*). Yet at the same time, Ashdown and his general election co-ordinator Des Wilson knew that their target seats were mainly Tory-held: any softening of approach towards Labour might scare off Tory/Liberal floating voters. Many Liberals retained unpleasant memories of the 1977-78 Lib-Lab pact and most felt a sense (probably unfairly) that the then Liberal leader David Steel had sold his Party short for little tangible gain.

Buoyed by a spectacular by-election win in Ribble Valley in March 1991, Ashdown decided to drive a hard bargain. He told the Liberal Democrat spring conference in Nottingham: 'Liberal Democrats will not participate in any government in the future, if that government turns its back on the need for electoral reform.' He told BBC radio listeners in April: 'I say to Mr Major and Mr Kinnock, "If that situation [a hung Parliament] comes about, don't even pick up the phone unless you are prepared to talk about a fair voting system".'[12] This was fighting talk from a Party with around 14 per cent in the opinion polls.

Paddy Ashdown's reaction to the interim Plant report was hostile: 'anyone looking for a real change in Britain, or justice in the British ballot box, will be feeling a profound sense of disappointment … Labour has failed to reach a conclusion … Labour has produced a smokescreen.'[13] In a telling criticism of Plant's distinction between 'legislative' and 'representative' institutions, Ashdown noted that 'under Labour, the more important an elected body, the less likely it is to be representative of public opinion.'

At the Liberal Democrats' autumn conference in a sunny Bournemouth in September 1991, Ashdown led his Party further down the road of free-market economics. Des Wilson and Party President Charles Kennedy made set speeches claiming Labour could not win the coming general election. Ashdown played down talk of a hung Parliament, preferring to concentrate on the Party's policies – although he rather ruined the effect by admitting to a group of journalists over dinner that he had been 'war-gaming hung Parliament scenarios' with close colleagues.

The Liberal Democrats' favoured form of PR is the Single Transferable Vote (STV). STV represents a greater threat to the interests of existing MPs that either AV or AMS, as it would remove significantly more Labour MPs in the north and Tory MPs in the south than any system retaining single-member constituencies in one form or another. Although STV is officially favoured by Conservative Action on Electoral Reform (CAER), it now has few adherents in the Labour Party – Jeff Rooker moved to the Additional Member System (AMS) during the deliberations of the Plant committee.

Official Liberal Democrat policy, in the words of a recent policy document, is 'the introduction of proportional representation for all elections including to the House of Commons, *preferably* by the Single Transferable Vote System' (my emphasis). Within the Scottish Constitutional Convention the Liberal Democrats have shown a willingness to compromise.

Ashdown consistently argued throughout 1990-92 that the Liberal Democrat price for support of a minority government would be electoral reform and an agreed programme for the full life of a Parliament. This is substantially more than was on the table either in the Heath/Thorpe negotiations in 1974 or in the Lib-Lab pact of 1977-78. It is a tough opening gambit.

A tricky, and more likely, scenario would be the greyer area of an offer from a larger Party of a Royal Commission or a constitutional convention. Proportional representation for any elected bodies would do much to raise the profile of the issue, and to expose the failings of First-Past-the-Post for the Commons. Any feasible change to the voting system, including the non-proportional Alternative Vote, would work to the Liberal Democrats' advantage, even if it upset the STV purists: and, at the same time, with a relatively small number of MPs, Ashdown's bargaining position is not strong. He has proved a formidable leader and has achieved an ascendancy over his Party greater than any Liberal leader since Gladstone. At heart he is a realist.

ROADS TO REFORM

The introduction of new elected bodies – a reformed second chamber, national assemblies in Scotland and Wales, regional assemblies in England – would provide a relatively painless opportunity for the introduction of proportional voting systems. The jobs of sitting MPs would not be on the line. But the sheer volume of legislation required to enact the changes, presumably in the face of determined opposition, suggests that the timescale for reform of the Commons may be at least two Parliaments.

The mechanism for reforming the Commons is also unclear. A straight manifesto commitment and whipped vote by one of the major parties is unfeasible. A post-election pact by either party with the Liberal Democrats is very unlikely to produce the 'moral mandate' for a whipped vote, and Commons arithmetic for a free vote looks very murky.

Royal Commissions have sometimes been the means to introduce innovative legislation, as they were in the reforming Liberal administration from 1906 to 1914. Just as often they have been suitable delaying devices, allowing the great and the good to deliberate at length while the politicians gradually move the goalposts. One was employed on electoral reform in 1910. An electoral convention on the Scottish model would have the advantage of placing an additional moral mandate behind MPs, tapping public support for change. It could help to bring reluctant MPs into the division lobbies.

Calculations of party advantage will remain important. Any change will have to be a compromise. Within the Conservative Party there are at least four potential groups of reformers: those who support proportional representation; those who have supported it in the past but whose interest has waned in office; those who support the Alternative Vote on merit, as does Emma Nicholson; and those, like John Biffen, who would support it as preferable to full PR. The majority of the parliamentary Party is likely to remain, for some time yet, sympathetic to the *status quo*.

Some have doubted whether Labour's interest in reform would survive office – 'Having got their cars and offices and so on, it would tend to be less important', suggests Conservative MP David Knox.[14] But a Labour government, or a Lib/Lab government, which pressed ahead with the establishment of elected assemblies for Scotland and Wales, and with the reform of the House of Lords, would be firmly on

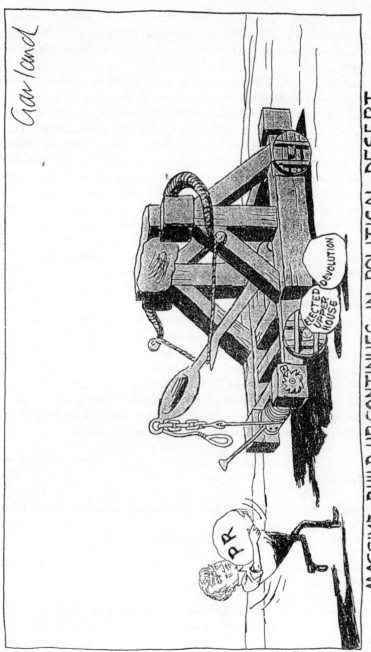

MASSIVE BUILD UP CONTINUES IN POLITICAL DESERT

Nicholas Garland, *The Independent*, 18 September 1990. © Nicholas Garland, 1990. Reproduced by kind permission.

the road of reform. European integration makes First-Past-the-Post less defensible and especially for European Parliament elections: as long ago as 1977, the majority of the Labour cabinet voted for PR for European elections.

The Plant commission has allowed the Labour leadership – Neil Kinnock, John Smith, Gordon Brown included – to retain an official 'open mind', and so given them an astonishing, and advantageous, room for manoeuvre on an issue of fundamental political importance. The majority of the parliamentary Labour party has simply kept out of the debate. Less than fifty MPs had 'come out' by the end of 1991, but, in the words of Austin Mitchell, 'there is a lot of hedging of bets.'[15] An NOP poll of seventy-eight Labour MPs for BBC TV's *On the Record* in January 1992 found thirty-nine (50 per cent) in favour of change, with twenty-seven (35 per cent) against, and twelve undecided or uncommitted. Over half were in favour of a constitutional convention.

Most prominent Labour reformers favour German-style AMS. Others have discreetly floated the 'Australian option': the introduction of the Alternative Vote for the Commons and STV or party lists for an enhanced upper house. Among the Labour MPs found to favour reform of Commons voting in the NOP survey, the Alternative Vote was significantly more popular than a proportional system. Any scenario for change will involve calculations about the intentions of both Tory and Labour reformers, and of the Liberal Democrats; the opposition of the Ulster Unionists to PR seems likely to continue, although the Scottish and Welsh nationalists support PR for independent national assemblies. Ironically, the fate of Britain's elderly voting system will be decided in smoke-filled rooms by the very politicians it has produced.

NOTES

1 Interview with G.S., for 'Level Spirits', *New Statesman and Society*, 19 July 1991.

2 Interview with G.S., for *Marxism Today*, October 1991.

3 Sir Ian Gilmour, *Inside Right*, Quartet, London 1978, p225.

4 Quoted in Trevor Russel, *The Tory Party*, Penguin, Harmondsworth 1978, p139.

5 Quoted in *ibid.*, p140.

6 Interview with G.S., for *New Statesman and Society, op.cit.*

7 Interview with G.S., for *Marxism Today, op.cit.*

8 *Ibid.*

9 Interview with G.S., for 'Dynamo Behind Voting Reform', *Birmingham Post*, 13 November 1991.

10 FPTP, quoted in Sarah Baxter, 'Self-Preservation', in *New Statesman & Society*, 19 July 1991.

11 Quoted in Ian Macwhirter, 'Labour Mends Split Over Electoral Reform', *Scotland on Sunday*, 15 December 1991.

12 Quoted in Patrick Wintour, 'Ashdown Tough Over Coalition', *Guardian*, 22 April 1991.

13 Paddy Ashdown, 'Ducking and Dithering', *Guardian*, 15 July 1991.

14 Interview with G.S., for *New Statesman and Society*, *op.cit.*

15 Interview with G.S., for Gareth Smyth (ed.), *Can the Tories Lose? The Battle for the Marginals*, Lawrence & Wishart, London 1991.

4

WHICH SYSTEM?

HELENA CATT

There are over seventy different ways around the world in which representatives are elected, but most of the variation comes from practical details. The different voting systems can be grouped into five main types, which I will explain in three stages.

First, I outline the general ways in which voting systems differ and explain the significance of these differences. Second, I explain the five basic systems: the Alternative Vote (AV), the Single Transferable Vote (STV), the Additional Member System (AMS), Party Lists, and First-Past-the-Post. Then I will examine some of the practical details.

Finally, I offer a consumer's guide to voting systems, and score each system on a variety of criteria.

THE GENERAL WAYS IN WHICH VOTING SYSTEMS DIFFER

Ballot papers are marked *either* with crosses (X), *or* with numbers (1, 2, 3 ...).

The way in which the ballot paper is marked indicates the degree of voter preference asked for. With an X voters are expressing only their primary preference. With numbers voters are being asked to rank the candidates from a range of parties in order of preference.

If voters are asked for minimal information, then the decision on first preference is more important. If you get only one chance to influence the result you may wish to guess how others will behave so that your vote can affect the result and is not wasted on a candidate with no chance of winning: you vote tactically. When more information is asked for, this prior guessing is not needed as your vote

28

will still be used if few others share your choice of first preference.

Giving preferences has other implications. Voters can vote for more than one party, which means that there is some incentive for parties to campaign more widely in the hope of picking up later preferences. (When preference voting is used in multi-member constituencies, voters must also decide between the candidates from within a party. This situation can lead to as much competition within parties as between them, possibly resulting in deep internal party rivalries.) Preference voting can also hinder party cohesion in that splinter parties do not run the same risk of splitting the vote: if a splinter party does not do well the later preferences can go back to the parent party.

So the way in which the ballot is marked determines the extent of choice given to voters, how often tactical voting is used and how the parties compete for votes.

The systems are based *either* on single-member constituencies *or* multi-member constituencies.

With single-member constituencies, all in that area are represented by the same person, who is meant to speak for everyone in the constituency. Voters have no choice about who to see about a problem, and the representative should in theory listen to all viewpoints. The representative must be attentive to all constituents to gain re-election, so links should be strong and elected representatives responsive.

In multi-member constituencies, while some may claim to speak for all, each representative may speak for a particular group within that area. Voters can choose which of the representatives to take any given problem or request to, and representatives will mainly deal with voters who have views similar to their own. Each representative is likely to be supported by a particular group, so will be responsive to its needs in order to gain re-election.

The effects on candidate selection in the two different types of constituency are also important, especially on the number of elected representatives from presently under-represented groups such as women and ethnic minorities. In a single-member constituency, each party puts forward one candidate; in a multi-member constituency, or where the party nominates a list, the party is more likely to field a balanced slate. For the selection of a single candidate the perceived 'safe option' tends to predominate – the white middle-class man.

However, when a list of candidates is needed for each party, it is prudent to have a balanced ticket.

Either **the systems are based on proportional representation (PR),** *or* **not.**

In a PR system, each party receives a share of the seats equivalent to their share of the votes: if it wins a tenth of the votes, it gets a tenth of the seats. Other systems are described as 'plurality' or 'majoritarian', based on the idea that in each area the person with the most votes should win (in majoritarian systems it has to be over half).

These differences have implications for the way parties campaign. Under a plurality system, each contest is a 'winner takes all, loser gets nothing' situation. So parties concentrate their energies in areas they have a good chance of winning and ignore other areas. This results in a vast number of safe seats, clustered representatives and targeted campaigning. In Britain, this clustering has now formed a rough north/south division in terms of MPs: excluding London, Labour won only three seats outside London in 1987 south of a line from the Wash to the Severn Estuary, while the Conservatives won only one of the fifteen seats in South Yorkshire.

When each contest is not 'winner takes all', parties must behave differently. If all parties have representatives in each area then all parties must campaign in all areas. The more difference that each individual vote makes to the overall number of representatives gained by that party, the more parties will campaign across the entire country and the more geographically spread will be the representatives of the different parties.

Under PR systems a party will gain a majority of seats only if it has a majority of votes. With a system that is not proportional, a government can make sweeping changes with the backing of less than half the voters.

THE BASICS OF EACH SYSTEM

First-Past-the-Post

The plurality system is used in Britain, Canada, New Zealand, India and the USA. The system evolved for an illiterate electorate, so an 'X' is used. Each area elects one representative who wins by gaining at least one vote more than any other candidate. Mid-term vacancies are filled by holding a by-election.

Table 4-1: The Systems on the Main Dichotomies

	FPTP	AV	STV	AMS	LISTS
Mark on ballot paper	X	1,2,3	1,2,3	X	X
Constituency type	single	single	multi	½ each	multi
PR or not	not	not	PR	PR	PR

FPTP = First-Past-the-Post
AV = Alternative Vote
STV = Single Transferable Vote
AMS = Additional member System
LISTS = Party Lists

The Alternative Vote (AV)

The Alternative Vote is a majoritarian system based upon the idea that a representative, in order to speak for the constituency, must have the backing of the majority of the voters. It is used for the Australian lower house. Each constituency elects one representative. Voters mark preferences against the candidates, a '1' for their favourite, a '2' for their next favourite, and so on until the voter no longer wishes to distinguish between the remaining candidates. The number of '1's for each candidate are counted: any candidate with over half the votes is elected. If this is not the case the candidate with the fewest votes is eliminated and the papers re-allocated according to second preferences. This continues until one candidate has received the backing of over half the voters. Any mid-term vacancies are filled by holding another election in that constituency.

Other majoritarian systems differ only in the way later preferences are collected. The Double Ballot, used in France, has two successive ballots. At the first ballot, voters place a cross beside their favoured candidate and anyone receiving over half the votes wins. If this does not happen the less popular candidates are eliminated (more popular candidates may also choose to withdraw) and the top two contenders then face a second ballot. The candidate with the most votes at this ballot wins the seat.

Under another variation, the Exhaustive ballot (as used by many trade unions in meetings), there are a series of votes. All candidates are voted for: anyone receiving half the votes wins, if this is not the case the bottom candidate withdraws and voters vote again. This process continues until one candidate has majority backing.

The main differences between the varieties is the way later preferences are collected. The consequence of this difference is the amount of information voters have before making subsequent selections. Under pure AV voters have no information on the behaviour of other voters, while in the modified systems of Double and Exhaustive ballots they have full information on how others divide across the candidates.

The Single Transferable Vote (STV)

This is a proportional system based on the idea that votes should be given to individual candidates rather than political parties. It is used in the Republic of Ireland, Malta, Tasmania and for the Australian Senate. STV was invented in the nineteenth century, simultaneously by Thomas Hare (an English statistician) and Carl Andrae (a Dane). John Stuart Mill, the great liberal thinker, was an early fan of this system. It is favoured by the Electoral Reform Society, the Liberal Democrats, and Conservative Action for Electoral Reform.

STV uses multi-member constituencies. Voters mark preferences for as many candidates as they wish – ranging from only one to all on the paper. A quota is used to determine the number of votes needed for a candidate to be elected. The most common method is the Droop quota (details below).

First preferences are counted and any candidate reaching the quota is elected. If a candidate has more votes than the quota those 'extra' votes are re-allocated to second preferences. Any candidate who has then reached the quota is elected. If there are still seats to be filled the candidate with the fewest votes is eliminated and those votes re-allocated to the next preferred candidate. This process continues until all seats are filled.

Variations used in other countries revolve around three key aspects: quota type; seat size; by-elections. I will look at the first two in the next section. Mid-term vacancies can be filled in one of three ways. There may be a new election in the whole constituency, or in just part of the constituency (if the representatives are seen as 'belonging' to a part of the area rather than the whole). In either case the by-election will be conducted by AV because only one person is to be elected. Alternatively the original ballot papers can be used to see which candidate would have been the next to be elected.

The Additional Member System (AMS)

This system was created by the Allies for use in West Germany after the Second World War. It was based on the British system with some modification to give proportionality. The overall result gives parties a share of the elected representatives equivalent to their share of the vote, while maintaining single-member constituencies.

Each voter has two votes: one for a candidate in the constituency and one for a party list (not necessarily the party of the candidate voted for in the constituency). Half the elected representatives come directly from the constituencies and the other half come from the lists.

In each single-member constituency a representative is elected by First-Past-the-Post. To compensate for the disproportionality which results, the Parliament is 'topped up' with representatives from party lists. These 'additional members' give an overall result which is proportional to the preferences expressed in the party-list voting. Any mid-term vacancies are filled by the next name on that party's list.

Several alternatives have been suggested, relating to the proportion that comes from the list, the number of votes given, the area covered by a list (regional or national), and how top-up MPs are selected. The Hansard Commission in 1976 suggested the removal of the second vote for a party; instead they would use the total number of votes each party received in the constituency elections. Any shortfall would be filled by the 'best losers' for that party. Another suggestion is that the constituency elections are conducted using AV, and again top-up members would be the 'best losers'; proportionality would thus refer to first preferences in the constituency elections.

Party Lists

This proportional system is based on votes for political parties rather than for individual candidates. It is used in most of continental Europe, including Finland, Norway, Czechoslovakia, Italy, the Netherlands and also in Israel and parts of South and Latin America. Each constituency returns a number of representatives. Parties put forward a ranked slate of candidates in each area and voters vote for one list. All votes for each party are totalled and all parties which cross an established threshold are allocated seats in a proportional manner. Parties then fill these seats with the people on their list, in descending order. Any mid-term vacancy is filled by the next candidate on that party's list.

Countries vary in the quota they use, the size of the threshold, the size of the constituency, and the ability of voters to change the order of candidates on the party list. All of these differences are dealt with in the next section. If not all seats are filled by a quota system (see below), some countries allow for the pooling of unused votes over a wider area. Alternatively, there may be a proportion of seats that are kept back for allocation after all the local results are in, to make the overall representation in the elected body proportional to the overall vote, perhaps compensating small parties who just missed out in several areas. In either case, the intention is to give greater overall proportionality.

PRACTICAL DETAILS

In going through the basic descriptions, it is clear that various details differ across countries that use the same system. Some of these details have also been touched on in the examples given of each system in practice. While they do not alter the basic idea of each system, the variations by which each system is implemented do have important political consequences.

Seat Sizes

The seat size, or number of representatives elected from that area, can vary greatly in multi-member constituencies. Israel and Holland treat the whole country as one constituency. For STV to work well, the ideal seat size is five, but this is not always possible, for instance in sparsely populated areas such as the Highlands and Islands of Scotland or in self-contained areas such as the Isle of Wight.

Party lists also work best with about seven representatives. At present, electoral areas are meant to keep communities intact. So, with different size electoral areas, the whole idea of constituencies representing communities and what constitutes a community would have to be addressed. There are important political consequences of differing seat size. In a four party situation, a three member seat might be seen as unfairly penalising one of those parties. A party that has geographically even support will do better the larger the seat area, while a party with geographically concentrated support will benefit from a seat whose boundaries closely coincide with that concentration.

Thresholds

A threshold that must be crossed before parties can gain

representatives is a feature of most systems that contain a party list. This is designed to keep out small parties. Two reasons are often given for excluding small parties: extremist ones are unwelcome; a plethora of parties will·lead to instability. In Germany it is 5 per cent in each region, in Sweden it is 12 per cent in the constituency or 4 per cent nationally. The level determines how big a small party must be before it gains representation. There is also the question of having national or regional thresholds, for instance would Plaid Cymru have to cross a UK 5 per cent threshold or gain 5 per cent of the votes in Wales? The size of threshold will also affect independent candidates, especially if it is a national threshold and independents cannot pool their votes together. The higher the threshold, the less proportional the overall result may be, as more votes may be excluded. It also means that more voters may be left without a representative they voted for, as their small party is excluded.

Quotas

A quota is used in all PR systems to determine proportionality. You would be forgiven for thinking that determining the proportion of seats each party gets would be easy: a quarter of the votes means a quarter of the seats and so on. The problem is with remainders. If a party has a quarter of the votes and there are forty-five seats, no problem, they get ten seats. But if there are forty seats, they get ten and a half seats, which is a problem. So different methods are used to determine who gets the last seat(s). This only relates to a few seats, but that could make a big difference to a small party. Some quotas tend to favour large parties and some small parties. The treatment of different size parties may also affect the likelihood of coalition government: favouring large ones may make it less likely, favouring small ones more likely.

The main quota systems used are d'Hondt, Droop, Hare and Sainte-Lague. D'Hondt quota works by giving a seat to the party with the highest average number of votes per seat won, at each round of the calculation. To calculate this, each party's vote is divided by the number of seats they have gained so far plus 1. So to begin with all are divided by 1 (0 + 1). The party with the highest average is given a seat so their vote is now divided by 2 (1 + 1) and the party which now has the largest average gets the next seat. This continues until all seats are filled. This tends to favour larger parties. Droop quota = [votes cast / (number of seats +1)] +1. A party receives a seat for each quota it can fill. Hare Quota = [votes cast/ number of seats] + 1. Each party who fills a quota receives a seat; extra seats are given to the party with the most votes not used. This is sometimes called the largest remainder system, especially when used for party list votes, and tends to favour smaller parties. Sainte-Lague quota is like the d'Hondt except that at successive rounds the party vote is divided by the next odd number (divisors are 1, 3, 5, 7 etc.). This also tends to help smaller parties. In the modified Sainte-Lague, the divisors are successively 3, 4, 5, 7, 9. This is better for small parties than d'Hondt but demands a higher vote before they begin to win seats.

While the arithmetic looks complicated, the basic ideas are simple. Both Droop and Hare set up a quota which must be filled, based upon the smallest number of votes needed effectively to fill the vacant seats. The other systems all look at the ratio between votes gained and seats won. The difference in calculation methods is due to different ideas about whether it is fairer to give big or small parties the last seat(s). Obviously, some take longer to count and so would prolong the agony for candidates on election night. But all are presently operated without problem.

Electoral Areas
Using the whole area or a sub area for top-up in AMS, and some forms of party lists, has implications for different types of parties. The area used is important in terms of where parties are weak and strong, and for parties that do not contest seats across the entire area. The larger the area that is used, the more accurate the proportionality will be as it encompasses more of the elected members. Using the larger area also gives a better spread for those parties that are supported across the area. However, if some parties are concentrated in smaller areas, they would benefit from having top-up related to that type of area and may lose out totally if a larger area were used.

Voter Preferences
The extent of voter preferences required can differ within all the alternative systems. For the preferential systems (AV and STV) some countries insist that all candidates are numbered while others will accept a ballot paper as valid if at least one candidate receives a preference. In Australia, voters may just mark a vote for a party and later preferences are given in the way indicated by the party prior to the election.

Within party lists, some countries allow voters to express a preference for particular candidates within the list and to change the order given by the party. The extent of preferences required from a voter has relevance for the time and ease of voting (and counting) and for who has most control over the personnel who enter the elected body. The less choice the voter is given, the quicker and easier it is to complete each part of the process. If voters can choose between candidates from within a party this means that intra-party competition will occur. It also means that a party cannot so easily ensure the election of groups not normally elected, if voters can decide to change the order.

VOTING SYSTEMS: A GUIDE FOR CONSUMERS

There is no easy answer to the question of which voting system to use: there is no universal agreement on what elections are supposed to do and different voting systems achieve different goals. This means that you have to look at the functions of the elected body, the expectations of those involved and the existing ideas about elections and representatives. Inevitably, compromises will be necessary as many desired objectives are mutually exclusive.

However, many of the qualities are on a sliding scale rather than being an either/or choice, so you need some idea of your ranked order of desirable qualities of a system. In the following table, I score the basic voting systems, as described earlier, in terms of some of the most common assets required from a voting system. All of these qualities have been mentioned in the previous text, as part of the different discussion, but I bring them all together here as a useful ready reckoner. The more stars in the box, the more that system will deliver the quality listed.

Table 4.2: Assessing the systems

	FPTP	AV	STV	AMS	LISTS
TECHNICAL ASPECTS					
Voting					
easy to vote	*****	***	**	****	*****
later preference used if favourite not win	no	yes	yes	no	no
can vote for more than one party	no	yes	yes	yes	no
voters held select which candidate(s) win for chosen party(ies)	no	no	yes	no	no
Candidates					
party can easily impose quotas					
– on candidates	no	no	yes	yes	yes
– on MPs	no	no	no	yes	yes
candidates from the same party compete	no	no	yes	no	no
independents can be elected	*	*	****	**	***
Seat allocation					
easy to count	*****	*	*	**	***
proportionality	*	*	****	****	*****
– constituency	*	*	***	*****	*****
– whole area covered by elected body			***	*****	
POLITICAL IMPLICATIONS					
Parties					
encouraged to win majority support	no	no	yes	yes	yes

	FPTP	AV	STV	AMS	LISTS
encourages party cohesion	yes **	yes ***	no ****	yes ***	yes ****
likely to mean coalitions	no *****	no ****	yes ***	yes **	yes ****
penalises small parties					
– geographically concentrated	**	*	*	*	*
– geographically spread	****	**	**	*	*
favours geographically concentrated parties	****	**	**	*	**
even geographic distribution of MPs from big parties	no *****	no ****	yes ***	yes ****	yes ****
likelihood of lots of safe seats	yes *****	yes ****	no ***	no ****	no ****
small extreme parties can be elected	*	*	**	***	****
Effect on Candidates					
aids election of women	*	*	****	***	****
aids election of ethnic minorities	*	*	****	***	****
personality voting likely	**	**	****	***	***
Strategies					
open to tactical voting	****	****	*	**	**
parties need only target some areas	*****	****	*	**	**
Effect of Political Relationships					
responsive local representatives	**	**	****	****	***
strong MP–electorate links	****	****	**	***	**

The more *'s there are, the more that system has of that attribute
FPTP = First-Past-the-Post
AV = Alternative Vote
STV = Single Transferable Vote
AMS = Additional Member System
LISTS = Party Lists

5

A VIEW FROM THE POLLING
BOOTH

TIM DAWSON

Discussion of the abstract workings of electoral systems and counting sheep perform a similar function for many people. With the hope of dispelling drowsiness, this chapter shows each electoral system as it would appear in the polling booth. The method of voting is graphically demonstrated, and the potential outcomes are predicted.

To illustrate the systems employing multi-member constituencies, new constituencies have been drawn up by amalgamating existing ones. The candidates shown in each example stood in the original constituencies in the 1987 general election. And the results have been worked out from the way that votes were cast in that election.

We cannot know how a different electoral system would have affected the way in which votes were cast in 1987. We can only guess how voters would have expressed multiple preferences, had they been allowed. The projected results, therefore, no more than illustrate how each system might work.

I have filled in the ballot papers by way of demonstration. The preferences expressed are not necessarily the editor's or my own.

FPTP in Practice
The country is divided into 650 constituencies, each represented by one MP.

Constituency: Bath, 1987

J.M. Dean (Al)	**X**
C.F. Patten (Con)	
J. Smith (Lab)	
D.N. Wall (Grn)	

To vote, you place a cross beside the name of the candidate you want to win.

The candidate in each constituency who receives the most votes (i.e. at least one vote more than any other) is elected MP.

Result:

	Votes	Percentage	
Patten (Con)	23,515	45.4	Elected
Dean (SDP/All)	22,103	42.7	
Smith (Lab)	5,507	10.6	
Wall (Grn)	687	1.3	

AV in Practice

The country would still be divided into 650 constituencies, each represented by one MP.

Constituency: Bath, 1987

J.M. Dean (Al)	3
C.F. Patten (Con)	
J. Smith (Lab)	2
D.N. Wall (Grn)	1

To vote, you place a number beside each candidate in order of preference. You can, if you wish, express only one preference.

To be elected, a candidate must gain at least 50 per cent of the total votes cast. In a seat where no candidate has over 50 per cent of the votes after the first preferences have been counted, the candidate with the least first preferences is eliminated. That candidate's second preferences are then added to the votes of the remaining candidates. In this example Wall would be eliminated first. His votes are not enough to take any of the remaining candidates over 50 per cent. At the next stage, Smith, the Labour candidate, is eliminated. If most of the voters who had put Labour (Smith) 1, put Alliance (Dean) 2, then Dean would have enough votes to win.

Result: The Alliance candidate would have beaten Conservative Chris Patten.

STV in Practice

Britain would be divided into 122 constituencies. Each would be represented by between two and six MPs. The new consituencies would be created by grouping together two to six of the existing constituencies. It is likely that the major parties would stand as many candidates as they thought they could win in each constituency.

Constituency: Strathclyde North (formerly Cumbernauld & Kilsyth, Monklands East, Monklands West and Strathkelvin & Bearsden); the candidates shown all stood in 1987, and the results have been calculated by adding together each party's votes in the original constituencies.

Constituency: Leicestershire West (formerly Blaby, Bosworth, Loughborough and Leicestershire North West).

Strathclyde North   *Leicestershire West*

J. Bannerman (All)	
K. Bovey (SNP)	3
T. Clarke (Lab)	8
C.S. Deans (All)	
S. Galbraith (Lab)	7
K. Gibson (SNP)	4
S. Grieve (All)	
M Hirst (Con)	
N. Hogg (Lab)	6
T. Johnson (SNP)	1
G. Lind (Con)	
J. Love (Con)	
A. McQueen (All)	
G. Paterson (SNP)	2
J. Smith (Lab)	5
A.E. Thompson (Con)	

D.G. Ashby (Con)	
D.C. Bill (All)	
S.J. Dorrell (Con)	
D.S. Emmerson (Con)	
R.G. Fox (All)	
D. Freer (Grn)	2
R. Gupta (Grn)	3
R.S. Hall (Lab)	6
N. Lawson (Con)	
R.E. Lustig (All)	
H.T. Michetschlager (Grn)	1
J.M. Roberts (Lab)	5
D.A.S. Tredinnick (Con)	
S.A. Waddington (Lab)	4
C.J. Wrigley (Lab)	7

You can express as many preferences as there are candidates by placing a number beside their name. In these four-member seats, many voters would place their first four votes (1, 2, 3, 4) for candidates of the party they most supported. The order in which they put them, however, would be up to them. John Smith, in Strathclyde North, would probably attract lots of first preferences as he is well known, though left-wing Labour voters might choose to place a first preference for a candidate who seemed more closely to represent their own views.

The total number of votes are counted (241,944 in Leicestershire West; 163,641 in Strathclyde North). This total is then divided by the number of seats in the constituency plus one to produce a 'quota' (for details of this and other quota systems, see below). To be elected, a candidate's votes must reach the same number as the quota. As with AV, if – when the first preferences are counted – four candidates do not reach quota, then the candidate with least votes is eliminated. Those votes are redistributed according to the second preferences. Similarly, if one candidate receives more votes than quota, their surplus votes are transferred. Candidates continue to be eliminated until four have been elected.

Result:

Strathclyde North: Labour 2, Conservative 1, Alliance 1. (Under FPTP Labour won all four seats.)
Leicestershire West: Conservative 2, Labour 1, Alliance 1. (Under FPTP the Conservatives won all four seats.)

Guessing a result like this can only be imprecise. In Leicestershire West the quota in this example was 48,389. Conservative candidates received 131,680 votes, Alliance candidates 54,218 votes and Labour candidates 54,160 votes. If the number of votes each party received is divided by the quota then it produces the result shown above. Labour and Alliance candidates would have received at least enough votes for one each of them to be elected. This assumes that most voters would have expressed preferences for all the candidates of whichever party they voted for. In Strathclyde North, the quota was 32,729. The Alliance only received 22,943 votes. They would only have won a seat if they received a significant number of the transferred preferences from the 19,686 people who voted SNP. Had those preferences gone to Labour, it is likely that they would have won a third seat.

AMS in Practice

The country would be divided into 325 constituencies each around twice the size of existing constituencies. Each constituency would be represented by one MP elected by First-Past-the-Post. The country would also be divided into eleven 'regions'. A further 325 MPs would be elected from party lists to represent each region. In this example,

East Anglia, there would be ten constituency MPs and ten MPs elected from party lists. Other regions may have more or less MPs, depending on their size.

Constituency: Norwich (formerly Norwich North and Norwich South).

Region: East Anglia (Cambridgeshire, Norfolk and Suffolk); as with STV above, the candidates shown all stood in 1987, and the results have been calculated by adding together each party's votes in the original constituencies.

Alliance	
Communist	
Conservative	X
Green	
Labour	
National Front	

J.L. Garrett (Lab)	
C.J.M. Hardie (All)	
H.P. Thompson (Con)	X

You have two votes. One for the MP to represent your constituency and one for a party. The party vote will be applied to the regional party lists of candidates to ensure that the representation of each party in Parliament is proportional to the vote it received across the whole region.

The votes for each constituency are counted much as they are now. If the two Norwich constituencies were merged, the Tories would easily win. Indeed, in East Anglia the Tories would win all ten constituency seats. The regional votes for political parties are then counted and the percentage of the regional vote each party received calculated. The ten party-list seats are allocated to ensure that the total number of MPs from each region accurately reflects the percentage vote they received. The parties would have published their lists prior to the election and candidates' names would be taken from the list in the order in which they appeared.

Result:
Norwich

Garrett (Lab)	34,662	
Hardie (All)	24,818	
Thompson (Con)	42,102	Elected

East Anglia

	Percentage votes	Constit seats	List seats
Conservative	52.1	10	1
Labour	21.7	0	4
Alliance	25.7	0	5
Others	0.5	0	0

Party Lists in Practice

The country would be divided into large constituencies, each returning between ten and twenty members. Each party would put forward a ranked list of candidates: the maximum permitted number of candidates on the list would be the same as the number of seats contested in a particular constituency. The constituency of Devon & Cornwall would have sixteen seats.

Constituency: Devon & Cornwall (formerly Exeter, Falmouth & Camborne, Honiton, North Cornwall, North Devon, Plymouth Devonport, Plymouth Drake, Plymouth Sutton, St Ives, South East Cornwall, South Hams, Teignbridge, Tiverton, Torbay, Torridge & West Devon, Truro); as with STV and AMS above, the results have been calculated by adding together each party's votes in the original constituencies in the 1987 general election.

Alliance	
Communist	
Conservative	**X**
Green	
Labour	
National Front	

You have one vote, which you use to express a preference for a particular party. Seats are awarded to the parties in proportion to the number of votes they secure, using the d'Hondt rule (see details of quotas on pp. 35-6) in each constituency separately. Candidates are elected in the order in which they appear on the list previously ranked by the party.

Result:
Devon & Cornwall

	Votes	Percentage	Seats
Conservative	428,368	48.8	8
Labour	113,420	12.9	2
Alliance	330,812	37.7	6
Others	5,788	0.7	0

(Under FPTP, Con 14, All 2, Lab 0)

6

SELLING THE SYSTEMS

THE ALTERNATIVE VOTE

PETER HAIN

The current First-Past-the-Post system is unfair and the case for electoral reform is strong. But the fatal defect of all the major proportional representation systems is that the scope for local accountability is undermined, and power is sucked upwards to regional or national levels of party structures.

The Single Transferable Vote (STV) system with on average five MPs in each 'multi-member' seat would mean monster constituencies (some covering hundreds of square miles), so breaking the historic link between the local electorate and the MP. List systems would favour candidates approved by the party machine, and local parties would lose virtually all influence. The Additional Member System (AMS) favoured by most PR advocates in the Labour Party would mean two classes of MP: some constituency-based, the others constitutional free-loaders chosen from lists and without any constituency responsibilities. Furthermore, each PR option has almost as many idiosyncracies as the current system, without its virtue of simplicity.[1]

Under PR the ordinary voter would also have less opportunity to determine the composition of the government, because coalitions will become the norm rather than the exception. This was acknowledged by the political scientist Sartori, a proponent of an 'elitist' system of democracy. He argued, quite unashamedly, that PR would be a good thing because it invariably produces coalition government which makes it difficult for the electorate to 'pin down who is responsible' for decisions! Another political scientist argued in similar terms that it would 'help protect the parliamentary Labour Party from extra-parliamentary control'. In the context of coalition governments, small parties usually hold the balance of power under PR, exercising an influence quite out of proportion to their popular support, as is the case, for example, in Germany and Israel.

A better option is the Alternative Vote (AV). Labour supported the AV in the period around and after the first world war and carried it through the House of Commons in 1931 before it fell in the Lords.

It is used in the Australian House of Representatives and retains single-member constituencies like the present ones. Rather than placing a mark against a single name, each voter numbers the candidates listed on the ballot paper in order of preference (e.g., 1st: Green; 2nd: Liberal Democrat; 3rd: Labour). If any candidate achieves an overall majority right away (i.e., more than half the first preferences of voters on the first count), then he or she is elected. If not, the candidate with the lowest number of first votes is eliminated and second preferences of voters for him or her are allocated to the other candidates as indicated. This process is repeated through later counts, with bottom candidates falling out at each stage and their votes allocated to those remaining until one of these achieves an overall majority.

The main advantage of the AV over the existing system is that it requires winning candidates to secure a majority of votes, and this is a major, if not complete, step towards meeting the criticisms made by PR supporters. Crucially, by maintaining single-member seats, it also maintains local accountability. But although it secures a fairer relationship between seats and votes, the AV is strongly opposed by supporters of PR, mainly because it does not achieve genuine proportionality.

Analysis of its impact by a London School of Economics study[2] suggests gains for Labour and the Liberal Democrats at the expense of the Tories, who benefit disproportionately from the current system. The study assumed opinion polls showing the two major Parties roughly level on about 40 per cent each.

The case for the AV is thus that:

- it is fairer than First-Past-the-Post;
- there is less scope for 'wasted' votes because electors could state their real first preference;
- there would be less geographical bias of the kind which now sees the Tories overrepresented in the South;
- each MP would have to secure at least 50 per cent of the vote;

- it is easier to form majority governments than under PR;
- the single-member seat would be retained;
- it is relatively simple, a virtue not without merit and which contrasts with the almost unfathomable complexities of most PR options;
- it does not require boundary changes, making it much easier and quicker to implement;
- by-elections would be easy to organise;
- it is also the only option the Commons would probably back, since MPs are hardly likely to vote themselves out of their own seats, and this highly practical matter should not be underestimated if the intention to reform is serious; one need only examine the debates and behaviour of MPs when the issue was last a major one in the post-first world war period to seek confirmation.

However, if the AV is adopted it should be in parallel to replacement of the House of Lords by a democratic second chamber elected under a List system of PR. This would enable the aspirations for completely proportional representation to be met in at least one half of Parliament while also producing a second chamber that could genuinely claim legitimacy as a constitutional check by containing as it would a fair spread of almost all political opinion from the Greens upwards.

It could be elected from party lists according to the regional vote their party polled in the same general election. The same vote given to a parliamentary candidate locally would be allocated to that candidate's party in a regional pool. The percentage of that pool received by each party would determine their allocation of 'Second Chamber' members from the region concerned. The objection to the List principle argued above does not apply in this case since members of the Second Chamber do not have any constituency duties or representative responsibilities.

It would also allow positive action to secure a fair represent tion of women, the regions and ethnic minorities. For example, the Labour Party could select its regional lists for the Second Chamber by democratic vote of either regional members or conferences, and we could build in quotas, thus satisfying legitimate claims for fair representation within the Party in a way that cannot be enforced whilst retaining local autonomy in selections.

By such an approach, we could retain the advantages of the single-member seat and the prospect of being able to form a single-party Government, with a reform of the Second Chamber which satisfied the demand for fairer representation. The adoption of the AV system thus forms the basis for a new agenda of electoral reform that is both credible and practical.

NOTES

1 For a detailed analysis and evidence see my *Proportional Misrepresentation*, Wildwood House, London 1986.
2 Stuart Weir and Patrick Dunleavy, *Independent on Sunday*, 29 September 1991.

The Additional Member System (AMS)

Jeff Rooker

There is no perfect electoral system. The interim report of the Labour Party working party on electoral systems, *Democracy, Representation and Elections*, has established that all electoral systems have advantages and disadvantages.

I serve on the Plant committee as someone committed to changing the voting system, but open-minded on which system to choose. I am now convinced of the thrust of the Plant report's analysis:

a) that there should be different electoral systems for the House of Commons and an elected second chamber, reflecting the different roles of the different chambers and preventing a clash of legitimacy in the event of disagreement;
b) that elections to the bodies which pass laws – such as the House of Commons and the proposed Scottish Parliament – should be 'community or constituency based'.

If party representation is broadly to reflect the votes cast, and the community or constituency base is to be retained, then only variants of AMS can meet the challenge. AMS combines the advantages of First-Past-the-Post and List systems. As a hybrid it is attacked by purists on either side of the reform debate. In its favour it must be recognised that AMS has commanded substantial support from considered analyses of voting systems, including the Hansard Society Commission on Electoral Reform (1976), and the 'Draft Constitution' published by the Institute for Public Policy Research (1991). The careful reader will also find support for AMS emerging from the Plant report.

I support an AMS system for the Commons and for a Scottish Parliament on the basis that:

- it is proportional to a degree;
- it is flexible;

- it is constituency based;
- it avoids wasted votes;
- it allows for a wide representation from a variety of occupational, social, denominational, religious, ethnic and gender backgrounds;
- it is simple to operate and to understand;
- it is fair to regions and in reflecting opinion;
- it is the only alternative to the *status quo* which can be phased in over time (should this be desired).

The unique flexibility of AMS in meeting a wide range of criteria makes AMS attractive to those of us who wish to preserve a strong constituency basis and achieve a much greater degree of proportionality than is possible under a plurality system such as First-Past-the-Post.

No one I know wants the Commons to be any larger than at present (651 MPs after the 1992 general election). As someone representing the largest constituency in Birmingham, with 20,000 more constituents than most urban MPs, I do not lightly advocate larger constituencies. But I have to consider the implications of electoral and constitutional reform and not treat larger constituencies in isolation from the overall benefits of AMS.

AMS is sometimes criticised on the basis that it throws up two classes of MPs – those elected in constituencies and those in the 'top up'. I once heard a parliamentary colleague eloquently argue that Privy Councillors (i.e. 'Right Hons') are a different class to the rest of us. The PCs have the right to have their letters answered personally by the Secretary of State, and the 'right' to be called early (in time for the television news) in debates. No PC ever resigns to join the rank and file of MPs!

In addition, ministers are extremely restricted in their ability to represent their constituents' interests. Under AMS members will be elected in different ways, but they will all be legitimate. The additional members will come either from highest losing candidates or from regionally selected party lists. There should be no role for lists drawn up by the parties' head office. If a party wants to enforce gender quotas (or indeed religious quotas), then the party list is the only way. But it would have to be a rigid list without voter control.

I take the view that the voters should have maximum control over who is elected. This presents a potential conflict with the enforcement of quotas through party lists. However, under a reformed electoral system a party will pay heavily if the balance of candidates is out of line. But it should be for the voter to decide if they want to elect members on a gender basis. Voter control of the list could be introduced by asking voters on the ballot paper to rank one party's list according to their own preferences. The overwhelming majority would rank the list of the party they support.

It is crucial that additional members should not be freeloaders. Constituency duties could be assigned either by parties or by an independent electoral commission.

It is also important that additional members should not be elected to a national Parliament unless their party has at least one constituency. This requirement puts real meaning into the word 'additional' and avoids the need for artificial, and therefore arbitrary, thresholds. If we believe in a system based on constituencies, then winning a constituency should be the threshold.

An election under AMS could be run in exactly the same way as under the present system, namely an 'x' on a ballot paper against a single name. The votes would be added up on a regional basis in order to elect the additional members. This would greatly reduce both the need and the temptation to vote tactically.

A practical advantage of AMS is that it would be phased in by gradually increasing the number of additional members, say to 20 per cent, 35 per cent and 50 per cent over three elections. This would minimise disruption and make change more acceptable to current MPs, but it is a bonus only if a 50:50 division is desirable. I am not certain that it is. The advantages of constituency representation have to be balanced against the advantages of proportionality.

A House of Commons of 450 or 500 MPs elected for constituencies with the remaining 200 or 150 elected as additional members would best meet the desired requirements. It would be fair to voters, balanced in terms of gender, ethnic religious representation, and proportional in the sense that seats won by parties would be broadly in line with votes cast. It is a long way from where we are now, but need not be too long in coming.

THE SINGLE TRANSFERABLE VOTE (STV)

ROBIN SQUIRE

Of all the widely used electoral systems, the Single Transferable Vote (STV) gives the greatest degree of choice to the voter. Essentially there are two separate aspects to the system, the first being that, like all systems of proportional representation, it ensures a Parliament elected broadly in line with votes cast. Unlike other PR systems, however, it does so without using party lists (in whole or part) or by creating two classes of MP, only one of whom has an identifiable constituency. For the important principle of retaining a specific geographical area or constituency is central to STV.

The second aspect is that voters have a choice of candidates instead of one per party, whether imposed by local or central party activists. In practice, each party would put forward one more candidate than the number of seats they expected to win in each constituency. Equally, because it would be in the interests of the parties themselves, there would be a significant increase in the selection of female candidates, on merit, and, particularly in many of our cities, candidates from ethnic minorities. As we have seen in other countries with proportional systems, this will lead in turn to a higher proportion of successful candidates being drawn from political minorities. Similarly, voters may choose between, for instance, socially conscious Conservative candidates and their right-wing colleagues; or between 'yuppy' socialists and those who still believe in their 1983 general election manifesto!

STV thus challenges head on the concept of single-member constituencies – and rightly so. It is a principle, sedulously fostered by MPs in particular, that one member per constituency is essential for democracy. What is the truth? To begin with, the identical principle is rejected in local government! Second, and clearly, the problem-solving aspects of an MP's job are not, usually, dependent upon the political party of the member concerned, although many constituents say openly that they prefer an MP of their own party handling their case.

On the political issues of the day, however, no one MP can represent the views of all his or her constituents. Where, for instance, were the MPs in (say) Surrey, Kent and Sussex who supported CND in the 1980s? Although I personally opposed their policies, a sizeable minority of unilateralists had no voice in the whole region. Similarly, who is speaking for the Government's Health Service reforms in (say) Glasgow, Liverpool or Manchester? We need a system which gives a large number of electors an MP who actually speaks for them rather than merely *claiming* to do so! It should also remove the present unhealthy dichotomy between a rural South and West with virtually no Labour representation outside inner London, and our major cities which contain little representation other than Labour! Some greater knowledge, among all political parties, of life in areas with which they currently have little contact would improve the body politic.

There are several other advantages from STV. In a typical five-member constituency, a candidate would need at least 10 per cent of the first preference votes to have a reasonable prospect of reaching the quota. This discourages the formation of very small parties and removes the need for a separate threshold. As with PR systems in general, coalition or minority government would often result, although countries and states using STV (i.e., Malta, Tasmania, Republic of Ireland) have found that a single party *can* have an overall majority. Nonetheless, it would usually deny a would-be government the chance to bring in the entirety of their programme unless they attract more than 50 per cent of the vote or reach accommodation with another party.

Perhaps as important, the thorny question of boundary revisions is minimised. A significant proportion of voters lose their existing MP *not* through a contested election, but by the operation of the Boundary Commissioners every fifteen years or so. This inevitably disrupts the relationship between MPs and their constituents. Under STV, constituencies are based on natural boundaries (away with Leeds South West, Leeds North East etc. and welcome Leeds!), with shifts in population being recognised by an increase or decrease in the number of MPs returned. Only major changes (e.g., the creation of new towns) should require boundary revisions.

All the above comments relate to Parliament, but it must be observed that STV is particularly suited to local council elections, where the concept of multi-member wards is well established. It would improve the quality of local government in many parts of the country if total domination of a council by one party were to cease.

The test of any system must be whether it works. Unlike the

Alternative Vote, STV does not carry a built-in bias in favour of the perceived 'middle' party whose larger number of second preferences would carry disproportionate influence. In practice that has produced parliaments in Australia as unbalanced as those using 'First-Past-the-Post'. In contrast, we know from experience abroad and from countless professional bodies here who have adopted STV that it produces properly balanced parliaments and assemblies. Indeed that is precisely why it has been introduced for elections to the European Parliament for Northern Ireland. Even in a country otherwise wedded to simple majority elections, the New York Academic Board is elected by STV in order that the range of opinions and backgrounds can be fairly reflected.

Under STV, on average, 80 per cent or more of electors help to elect a constituency MP of his or her choice. This compares, for instance, with the 1983 general election where more votes were cast for *losing* candidates than were cast for MPs elected! Enabling most electors to play a positive part in electing an MP is not the least attraction of a system whose adoption is long overdue.

7

THE THOUGHTS OF JO PUBLIC: OPINION POLLS AND ELECTORAL REFORM

GARETH SMYTH

Opinion polling on electoral reform shot to prominence in 1991 through a tactic used by the Electoral Reform Society. At a crucial time in Labour's internal debate, the ERS commissioned a poll to ask Liberal Democrat voters how they would vote if Labour backed proportional representation, and 21 per cent said they would switch to Labour. It was a startling finding.

Around the same time, a MORI 'State of the Nation' poll for the Joseph Rowntree Reform Trust suggested that half the electorate favoured a change to proportional representation, with less than a quarter against. The poll took electoral reform into the pages of the *Sunday Mirror*, and was hailed elsewhere as 'mould-breaking' by two enthusiasts who claimed it revealed 'the making of a popular democratic front that Labour is well-placed to lead, raising the party's own electoral appeal, outflanking the Liberal Democrats and isolating the Tories'.[1]

'IT DEPENDS HOW YOU ASK US'

Other commentators were less convinced. Peter Kellner, writing in the *Independent* ('Do We Favour Reform? It Depends How You Ask Us', 24 May 1991), suggested that the MORI poll had been based on the 'fallacy of the cost-free benefit': the pitfalls of PR had not been pointed out. Voters may like the idea of 'proportional representation' but will become less favourably disposed once 'disadvantages' are pointed out.

Kellner commended the polling of NOP, which he had played a role in devising. NOP had counterposed two propositions which expressed the 'advantages' of both alternatives. The results suggested public opinion was more evenly balanced than the 'State of the Nation' poll portrayed (see Table 7.1).

Table 7.1   NOP poll for Newsnight/*Independent*

	06.90	04.91	01.92
We should change to a system of proportional representation so that the number of MPs for each party reflects the number of votes it gets across the whole country:	57	45	51
We should keep to the present system of 'First-Past-the-Post' to produce an effective government by the largest party:	34	46	39
Don't know	9	9	10

The poll of May 1991 suggested there had been a *drop* in support for PR – at the very time of the 'mould-breaking' MORI polling. In fact, as pointed out by John Curtice, the NOP question of May 1991 may have received a different response simply because it was prefaced by a different question:

> This asked 'At present, the candidate who wins the most votes in an election becomes the MP. How satisfied or dissatisfied are you with this system of choosing MPs?' Faced with this characterisation of the existing system, 62 per cent indicated their satisfaction with it. Having done so, it is not surprising that rather fewer supported PR.[2]

Gallup asked this same question in 1983 and twice in 1985, finding between 58 and 61 satisfied and between 31 and 39 dissatisfied. This high level of satisfaction may be attributed to voters responding quickly to something that seems 'fair', or it may reflect the attraction of a single representative for an area. When MORI polled in January 1992, the question was not asked before the PR/First-Past-the-Post alternatives were posed, and responses to the latter returned to roughly where they had been in June 1990 (see Table 7.1). Such sensitivity is telling evidence that voters do not have a considered view of different electoral systems.

This is not uncommon in opinion polling. It is an established adage of opinion pollsters that voters often want contradictory things – for example, lower taxation *and* higher spending on public services. Robert Waller, Director of Political and Social Research at Harris, is sceptical of much of the polling on electoral reform:

> People want to be positive, to say yes rather than no, and to say satisfied rather than dissatisfied. They will tend not to oppose an idea unless it seems actively unattractive, so can be seen to support contradictory positions simultaneously. By far the best questions are those which pose alternatives, though the descriptions of matters unfamiliar to most voters are often biased or confusing.[3]

Unfortunately, the pollsters have generally asked different questions over time, making it difficult to draw general conclusions about changes in public opinion. Between 1985 and 1988 Gallup counterposed 'fairness to smaller parties' with 'effective government'. In fact First-Past-the-Post can favour small parties if they are geographically concentrated: the use of the word 'effective' is perhaps loaded, but is at least common to the NOP polling.

Table 7.2   Gallup

Some people say we should change the voting system to allow smaller parties to get a fairer share of MPs. Others say we should keep the voting system as it is to produce effective government. Which view is closest to your own?

	01.88	05.87	10.86	12.85
Change	38	35	35	45
Keep it as it is	51	56	57	47
Don't know	11	9	7	8

Comparing the Gallup figures (Table 7.2) with the NOP (Table 7.1) might suggest that public support for electoral reform had increased substantially (from around 38 per cent to around 51 per cent) between the late 1980s and the early 1990s. But, just as likely, the figures are produced by the different 'benefits' of reform referred to in the questions. Seats won being 'proportional' or 'reflecting the number of votes' is apparently a more attractive reason to support reform than 'fairness to small parties'. When Gallup asked in November 1985 'Would you be in favour of a system where the number of seats won in the House of Commons was proportional to the number of votes won nationally?', 59 per cent of the sample said 'yes', and only 20 per cent 'no'. But neither question seems able to gauge accurately an *overall* view of whether the voting system should be reformed: as Kellner put it, 'it depends how you ask us'.

A poll carried out (in the different political circumstances of September 1975) by the Opinion Research Centre for the *Evening Standard* combined 'fairness to small parties' and 'proportionality' in its questioning. It found an even spread of views. 45 per cent agreed 'we should change the present system of voting because it is unfair to the smaller parties, and means that the number of seats a party wins in Parliament may have little connection with the number of votes it gets'. 43 per cent agreed that 'we should keep the present system of voting, although it is unfair to the smaller parties because it is the best way to get majority governments to take the strong measures necessary to tackle the country's problems'.

When asked baldly – 'Are you in favour of proportional representation?' – the public has generally said 'yes'. It does, after all, sound like a good thing. A 1977 MORI poll for the *Sunday Times* found that 43 per cent were in favour of PR, and 20 per cent against. Bigger majorities have been found for more favourably phrased questions. In March 1974, just after a general election produced a hung Parliament, 70 per cent questioned by the Opinion Research Centre thought it would be 'a good idea' if the number of seats won by a party in a general election reflected the number of votes won. In 1977 a Marplan poll for the *Sun*, eliminating 'don't knows', found 72 per cent of voters agreeing that proportional representation was 'most fair to voters' with only 28 per cent feeling the same about the present system.

There have been some exceptions to the general pattern of support. A Marplan poll in September 1982 asked: 'Do you think the present voting system should be changed so that parties in the House of Commons would get a share of the seats more closely in line with the proportion of votes cast for them, or do you prefer the present system?'. 49 per cent said they preferred the present system, with 45 per cent opting for change. This contrasted sharply with a Marplan poll taken only seven months earlier: in January 65 per cent had expressed support for PR and 58 per cent for coalition government. The turnaround was remarkable.

This 1982 polling suggests an important factor in voter attitude to electoral reform. In January Mrs Thatcher's Conservative government was highly unpopular. By September, the political situation had been transformed by the Falklands conflict which, it seems reasonable to conclude, strengthened support for 'strong, single-party government' and thus for First-Past-the-Post. Voter perception of the particular single-party government in office influences voter attitude towards change. This may help to explain the increased support for First-Past-the-Post recorded in the April 1991 NOP poll (see Table 7.1): not only had John Major replaced Mrs Thatcher and so revived Conservative fortunes, but the new Prime Minister had successfully led the country through the Gulf war.

A more difficult poll to explain in such terms is a Marplan poll for the Press Association published in November 1986, at a time when the Conservative government was roughly level with the Labour opposition in the polls. 43 per cent favoured proportional representation, with 49 per cent against: 45 per cent expressed a preference for coalition government, with 50 per cent against.

'Working Together'

The Marplan finding was unusual. There has been generally much less support for coalition government than for PR, although the former is a likely consequence of the latter. A 1989 NOP poll found 58 per cent in favour of PR, but 54 per cent agreeing that 'government by a single party able to rule on its own' was 'best for Britain'. The 1975 Opinion Research Centre poll for the *Evening Standard*, found more in favour of 'fairness' than 'coalition':

MORI asked in September 1989 'Which do you think would be best for Britain – government by a single party able to rule on its own, or government by two or more parties working together?'. 54 per cent said a single party and 39 per cent two or more parties. When MORI asked the same question in January 1992 the position had reversed: 46 per cent favoured a single party and 48 per cent two or more parties. All this suggests a slight increase in public support for coalition, but the differing questions asked by pollsters over the years make conclusions speculative.

"*We can't ALL be opinion pollsters?*"

Nick Newman, *Private Eye*, 27 September 1991. © *Private Eye*, 1991.
Reproduced by kind permission.

Table 7.3   ORC

Do you think it would be a good idea or a bad idea if a new system of voting were brought in –

	Good	Bad	Don't know
so that the number of seats a party wins in an election reflects the number of votes it gets?	66	17	17
which would make coalition governments more likely and government by the Labour or Conservative parties alone less likely?	44	34	22

There can be little doubt, however, that PR is not regarded by voters as an important issue in itself. It has never figured on the pollsters' prompted question about factors shaping the way people vote. Significantly, however, when the 1991 'State of the Nation' poll asked how the system of government could be improved – a question bent towards constitutional factors – 28 per cent went for the abolition of the poll tax and 14 per cent for the improvement of the NHS; only 12 per cent specifically mentioned PR.

Electoral reform is a subject most voters have little knowledge about. Polling by MORI for the Electoral Reform Society has found between 39 and 54 per cent of the electorate have either never heard of proportional representation or do not know what it is. Only around a quarter claimed to know 'a great deal' or 'a fair amount' about PR (see Table 7.4). The professed level of ignorance was much higher than suggested in the numbers of 'don't knows' in other polling about electoral reform.

Given the inconclusive nature of polling on electoral reform, any attempt to make generalisations about groups within the population – women, young people, or the 'chattering classes' – must be extremely tentative. Unsurprisingly, the professional classes, the A/B groups are more likely to claim knowledge of PR than Ds and Es. The A/B groups are more likely to support proportional representation but *less* likely to support coalition government. Break-downs by region and by age produce no clear pattern, with different polls producing different results.

Table 7.4 MORI

Would you say you know what is meant by the term proportional representation when applied to parliamentary elections, or not? If yes, how much would
you say you know about the term proportional representation or PR used to
describe an electoral system?

	08.89	08.90	05.91
A great deal	5	5	5
A fair amount	18	19	20
Just a little	23	37	31
Never heard of it	19	25	31
No, don't know the meaning	35	14	13

An NOP poll in January 1992 found higher support for PR among
men than women (53 per cent to 50). Women were, however,
significantly more in favour of 'government by two or more parties
working together' (52 to 43) – 51 per cent of men, as against 41 per cent
of women, preferred 'government by a single party able to rule on its
own'. An NOP poll in 1989 had found similar results on coalition, but
that 61 per cent of women, as against 54 per cent of men, favoured PR.

Generally, PR seems to be more popular with men than with
women. Women are more likely to favour coalition, and more likely to
say they 'don't know'. 55 per cent of women told MORI in April 1991
they 'hadn't heard of' or 'didn't know the meaning of' PR, compared
with 32 per cent of men. Similar discrepancies had been found in 1990
and 1989.

'HOW WOULD YOU VOTE IF...'

The influence of views on proportional representation on voting
behaviour is far from clear. Liberal Democrat voters are significantly
more likely to favour change than either Labour or Conservative
voters: since 1979 Labour voters have favoured change more than
Conservative voters, but when Labour was in government in the 1970s
the position was reversed. This suggests that a voter's views on PR may
be a consequence rather than a cause of voting intention. Care needs to
be taken in drawing any conclusions from 'switch' questions ('How
would you vote if Labour supported ...?') because they invite the

respondent to concentrate solely on one issue. 32 per cent of Liberal Democrat supporters told Harris in September 1991 that a Labour commitment to PR would make it 'more likely' they would back Labour, with 62 per cent saying it would make no difference. Similar findings came in Gallup polls.

Table 7.5 Gallup

If before the next election the Labour Party said that, if it won the election, it would change the voting system and introduce proportional representation for future elections, would that make you more inclined to vote Labour, or less inclined, or would it make no difference?

	01.92	09.91	08.91
More inclined	25	25	24
Less inclined	10	6	8
No difference	60	63	62
Don't know	5	5	6

21 per cent of Liberal Democrat voters *told* MORI in 1991 they *would* switch to Labour if Labour backed PR, but this does not mean they all would in practice. A series of 'switch' questions asked at the same time on different issues (electoral reform, the health service, defence, Europe etc.) would presumably produce different totals for different parties. It is the mixture of issues which shapes the basic decision taken by the voter in the election about where to place the cross on the ballot paper.

A remark by Robin Cook suggests an additional reason why support for PR could benefit Labour – 'It could be a powerful part of sending out a signal that the Labour Party is genuinely interested in creating an open and democratic society.'[4] Despite the transformation of the party under Neil Kinnock voters still retain significant fears: a Harris poll in September 1991 found 27 per cent of Liberal Democrat supporters and 43 per cent of Conservative supporters thought Labour 'would give too much power to the trade unions'. 46 per cent of Liberal Democrat supporters, 50 per cent of women, and 56 per cent of young voters thought Labour had 'just changed to win the election': overall, only 42 per cent of the electorate thought Labour had 'really become more moderate'. Robin Cook's remark hints at the important political consequences which could flow from Labour abandoning First-Past-the-Post: a commitment to PR could be taken as a sign that Labour was prepared to renounce single-party government in order to

Tony Hannan, *Bradford Telegraph & Argus*, June 1991. © Tony Hannan, 1991. Reproduced by kind permission.

allay residual public concerns which blighted the Party in the 1980s – the image of incompetent 'loony left' councils and political extremism, and the fears of trade union power.

The results of a referendum on a change in the electoral system cannot be taken for granted. The political circumstances in which it took place would be important. There was polling evidence of majorities against Britain's membership of the European Community between entry in 1973 and the 1975 referendum; yet the 'yes' campaign, backed by the leaderships of all three parties and by Fleet Street, won relatively comfortably.

A referendum on electoral reform where all three parties backed a certain change would be likely to tap the general public support. A referendum on a proposal backed by one or two parties in Government, and opposed by an opposition articulating the 'disadvantages' of change would be altogether more problematic and might hinge on the general popularity of the Government.

It is also far from clear whether public airing of the issues around electoral reform would lead to more or less support. Most voters do not claim any great knowledge about electoral reform. They tend to believe seats should be proportional to votes, but are less concerned about 'fairness' to small parties. There is scepticism about coalition, but views are fluid: experience of coalition government is, after all, limited to the 1977–78 'Lib-Lab' pact when the Government was already unpopular (there has been no other peacetime coalition in this century other than the emergency 'National Government' formed in the economic crisis of 1931).

If increasing tactical voting and declining voter turnout (from 84 per cent in 1945 to 75 per cent in 1987) reflect disillusionment with the political system, there is little concrete polling evidence that this has been turned in a definite direction by electoral reformers. Changing the electoral system would be a sea-change for the whole political system in Britain – the reformers have yet to convince voters this would be in their interests.

NOTES

1 Stuart Weir and Patrick Dunleavy, 'Left for Rights', *New Statesman & Society*, 26 April 1991.
2 John Curtice, 'Not Such a Big Idea', *New Statesman & Society*, 6 September 1991.
3 Robert Waller, comment to the author.
4 Robin Cook, interview with G.S. in *Marxism Today*, October 1991.

8

THE SCOTTISH EXPERIENCE
IN PROPORTION

PETER JONES

Discussing political prospects in late 1991, a senior Scottish Labour MP remarked that he thought 1992 would be one of the most significant dates in British history this millenium. He wasn't talking about 1992 as the year in which the European Single Market opened for business, or as the year in which the British Government finally climbed aboard the European train. This MP, known as a hard-headed pragmatic thinker neither to the left nor the right of the party, thought that 1992 would be as significant as 1707.

1707 was the year that Scotland's Parliament decided to join England's Single Market, signed up for a British single currency with a hundred-year transition period in which banknotes had both Scottish and English pounds printed on them, voted itself out of existence and then went for a good dinner. It is odd that what was apparently so good for Scotland is now so bad for the UK.

He thought 1992 would be significant, not just as the date on which a Labour Government re-established that Scottish Parliament, but as the year in which a process was begun that would eventually lead to a wholesale constitutional reform as historically important as the Treaty of Union. It would lead to the abolition of the House of Lords with its centuries of ossified tradition and its replacement by an elected second chamber; to replacement of the centralised state by a decentralised state with regional governments; and to the final discrediting of First-Past-the-Post as an electoral system and its replacement by proportional representation.

The fulfilment of that agenda, of course, would be dependent on the outcome of the 1992 general election. But from any political perspective, the present structure of government is under more pressure than for generations. The strength of the Charter 88 movement which continues to grow rather than decline is part of that pressure. The European dimension which constantly threatens to pull the Conservative Party apart, as it would also put strain on a Labour Party in government, is another pressure.

THE LION RAMPANT

And then there is the Scottish question. Once more the head of the Lion Rampant is poking above the parapets of Westminster, peering into the chamber of the House of Commons, occasionally giving a roar as it did in the Kincardine and Deeside by-election and the Glasgow Govan by-election before that, each time causing the denizens of that place to rush around in panic.

Of course, it can be argued that we have seen all this before. Was the roar of the Lion in the North not heard in the 1970s? And when it was asked what it wanted, didn't the roaring turn into coughing and spluttering and the lion into a mouse?

That's what happened in the 1979 devolution referendum. But the context was entirely different. The 1970s were a time of world economic upheaval caused by the oil price shocks and the shift in traditional manufacturing power from the cradles of the Industrial Revolution to the new industrial powers of the far east. The Scottish National Party offered a constitutional escape route via North Sea oil wealth from what was really an economic argument between the ideologies of left and right, with the right eventually emerging triumphant.

The 1990s, however, are a time of constitutional upheaval. Through the dust clouds of the demolished Berlin Wall can be seen nations arising of which most people have never heard – like Slovenia and Croatia; or nations that most people thought were Ruritanian historical curiosities – like Lithuania, Estonia, and Latvia. Even in apparently stable western Europe, there is constitutional upheaval: at the macro-level of rewriting the Treaty of Rome; and at the micro-level in, for example, Belgium. Can anyone predict whether or not Belgium will split into Flanders and Wallonia by the time the millenium is out?

It is impossible to conceive of the United Kingdom being untouched by these events. Especially now that the economic argument between left and right has been confined into a narrow spectrum, the stage is set for British political debate to move onto wider constitutional ground. Here the Conservative Party is badly positioned, for resistance to constitutional change is, in the ultimate, a defining text for most Conservatives. 'What is Conservatism?' asked Abraham Lincoln. 'Is it not adherence to the old and tried, against the new and untried?'

Margaret Thatcher was an economic radical, but a constitutional reactionary. Her reaction to the constitutional pressure of Europe – 'No, No, No!' – led directly to her downfall. And her reaction to the constitutional pressures of Scotland has left her Scottish Conservative Party with an equally deadly legacy.

For anyone wanting to hazard guesses as to where a British constitutional debate will lead, then the outcome of recent political debate in Scotland provides some very good pointers, one being that electoral reform leading to proportional representation is now odds-on. Some have already drawn that conclusion. The Liberal Democrat leader Paddy Ashdown, on most of his many visits to the Kincardine and Deeside hustings, declared happily: 'Where Scotland leads, the rest of Britain will surely follow.' That the Labour Party in Scotland, at a time when it had never had more support from the Scottish electorate, chose to form a political partnership with the Liberal Democrats and so came to accept the case for electoral reform, must rank as an extraordinary development.

It came about because, in victory, a crisis was born. The victory was Labour's capture in 1987 of fifty of Scotland's seventy-two parliamentary seats, compared to the Conservatives' humiliating loss of eleven seats and reduction to only ten MPs with which to govern Scotland. But it was Labour, not the Tories, who were then faced with a crisis. As the Tories' Scottish manifesto had been rejected by the Scottish electorate (the Conservative vote dropped from 28 per cent in 1983 to 24 per cent in 1987), people began to ask: what mandate did they have to rule Scotland?

The poll tax gave the 'no mandate' question real meaning. Labour activists began to talk the language of nationalism, even if they did not regard themselves as nationalists. Labour MPs discussed and tried out parliamentary 'guerrilla' tactics. Constituency activists launched in March 1988 a new fringe group – Scottish Labour Action. It was committed to getting a Scottish Parliament established irrespective of whether Labour won the following general election, and to civil disobedience aimed at bringing down the poll tax by a mass campaign of non-payment. (At a special conference in September 1988, in Govan Town Hall, mass non-payment was defeated, but only just. Labour's leaders had reluctantly to settle for a policy which left it to individual consciences whether they paid or not.)

Against this turbulent background, Labour's Scottish leaders, which effectively meant the shadow Scottish Secretary Donald Dewar and the Party secretary Murray Elder, had to work out how to channel activist energies in a more constructive way than campaigning for poll tax non-payment. Both were more committed to devolution than any of their predecessors, and recognised that the Party wanted more than had been achieved since 1987 by the usual means of demonstrations, policy up-dating, and Commons debates.

THE CONSTITUTIONAL CONVENTION

Back in 1979, days after the referendum, a small group formed the cross-party Campaign for a Scottish Assembly, aiming to keep the whole idea alive. It campaigned desultorily until after the 1987 election, when an idea conceived some years earlier came into play. The CSA had borrowed from history the notion of a Constitutional Convention, a mechanism sometimes created by governments and sometimes by force of circumstances, but which in either case brings together the leading elements of society with the aim of creating a new political settlement.

The CSA commissioned seventeen more or less eminent Scots under the chairmanship of Sir Robert Grieve, a former chairman of the Highlands and Islands Development Board, to produce a report, *A Claim of Right for Scotland*, which was published in July 1988. Its elegant prose and argument created considerable political stir.

Essentially, it contended that between the wishes of the Scottish electorate and the workings of the political system there was a gap, a democratic deficit, to coin a phrase. It called for a Constitutional Convention of the Scottish political parties, the trade unions, businesses, the churches, local authorities, and other interests to be convened to devise a more satisfactory political settlement.

The Conservatives were as dismissive as the Liberal Democrats were enthusiastic. Labour was cautious, talking about months of consultation and possibly a decision at the March 1989 conference. The SNP were suspicious, and laid down certain conditions of participation, drawn from their party policy which clearly called for an elected Convention.

The Labour Party, because of its parliamentary strength, its dominance of the local authorities and the trade unions, was crucial to the enterprise. Whatever doubts Donald Dewar had about going into the Convention were dispelled by the Govan poll tax conference. The way non-payment had pushed to the top of the Scottish Party's preoccupations alarmed him, for it suggested a rapid slide into nationalism was possible.

In a significant speech on 21 October 1988, at Stirling University, Dewar swept Party proprieties to one side and announced that Labour would play a constructive role in the Convention. He acknowledged that the Convention was an extraordinary extra-parliamentary route to take: 'It is based on the assumption that it is possible to mount pressure even on a hostile administration and that there are tactics other than simply working for national victory at the next election.' He acknowledged also that it was a gamble: 'What we have got to do is to persuade Scotland that fear must be conquered and canny caution be put on one side. The people must decide if they are prepared to live a little dangerously in order to achieve what they want.'

The people responded unexpectedly quickly a month later when they converted a 19,000 Labour majority into a 3500 SNP majority in Glasgow Govan, electing Jim Sillars, whose use of his exceptional talents in the nationalist cause against the party of his upbringing has made him particularly hated by Labour. His election in a heartland seat was a galvanising shock to Labour.

Dewar's decision to go into the Convention was thus entirely justified even if the outcome could not be predicted. 'We knew it was taking a tiger by the tail, but what the hell, we thought we might as well grab on and enjoy the ride,' said a colleague. To those who know Dewar, that will sound uncharacteristic. But these were uncharacteristic times.

The Nationalists and the Conservatives, neither wishing to be contaminated by what was always going to be aimed at legislative devolution, stayed away. Nevertheless, the turn-out at the first meeting of Convention in the historic setting of the Assembly Hall of the Church of Scotland in Edinburgh was impressively wide. Out of seventy-two MPs eligible to attend, fifty-three were present, plus three of the eight Euro-MPs. Ten of the twelve regional and island councils were represented, as were forty-two of the fifty-three district councils. Other political parties included the Communists, the Co-op, the

Greens, and the Orkney and Shetland Autonomy Movements. The churches, the Scottish Trades Union Congress, and some interest groups such as *Commun na Gaidhlig* (Gaelic Council) were represented. The Convention met a further five times, and apart from a rather purposeless meeting in Inverness, attendance levels have stayed at much the same levels. Most of the real work has been done by working groups of a thirty-member executive committee chaired patiently by an Episcopal churchman, Canon Kenyon Wright.

Canon Wright has given the Convention its one moment of public theatre – the triumphant roar of approval at that first meeting which greeted his answer to his rhetorical question as to what the Convention would do when Mrs Thatcher said 'No' to their proposals: 'Well, we say yes, and we are the people!'

That moment of vision apart, the Convention's work has been a long, hard, slog through thickets of financial systems and quagmires of powers, with the route-maps showing that the most difficult terrain to cross would come near the end of the trail and was called electoral reform.

The Liberal Democrat position was set out succinctly in a press statement issued by the Scottish Party leader Malcolm Bruce on 4 March, 1989:

> If a Scottish Parliament is not to replicate the worst excesses of the Westminster system, it must be radically different. The crucial ingredient is the voting system. It must be elected by a genuinely fair and representative form of proportional representation.
>
> To replace the government of Scotland by a Conservative dictatorship based on only 42 per cent of the UK votes and 24 per cent of the Scottish vote, will be resisted all the way by Social and Liberal Democrats. It would in any case be quite unsellable in our areas of strength in the Highlands and Islands, the rural areas of north-east and central Scotland, and the Borders.

This last point brings out one of the central motifs of Scottish politics. It is now generally accepted that the principal reason for the failure of the 1979 devolution proposals to reach critical mass was internal *division*: there were Labour No and Labour Yes campaigns; Conservative No and Conservative Yes campaigns. It is also a general perception that rural Scotland said No to devolution, and urban Scotland said Yes. It is certainly true that in Strathclyde region 54 per cent voted Yes, and in Orkney & Shetland only 27 per cent voted Yes. But in Highland region, 51 per cent voted Yes compared to 50 per cent voting Yes in Lothian region.

The crucial watershed of opinion here is not between city and country dwellers, but between differing perceptions of Scottish political futures based on the 1918 episode of workers' ferment called Red Clydeside, a sacred icon of Scottish socialism in west central Scotland. But in the east of Scotland outside the mining areas of Lothian and Fife, Red Clydeside is part of the demonology which Conservatives wave in front of voters of a more individualist tradition. 'A Scottish Parliament means rule by Glasgow trade unionists' is not as pithy as 'Home Rule Means Rome Rule', but it has much the same effect on the target audience.

The Liberal Democrats, who then held all four Highland seats, the Orkney & Shetland seat, both Border seats, the rural Fife seat, and one seat in Grampain (two after November 1991), had the best claim to speak for rural Scotland. Their belief is that proportional representation bridges the divide between the collectivist and individualist outlooks, promising each no more and no less than its due in a Scottish Parliament.

LABOUR SAILS ACROSS THE CLYDE

Why should Labour, so dominant in Scottish politics, have paid any attention to this? Indeed, the hardness with which the Liberal Democrats should push their PR demands was the major issue at their Scottish conference in March 1990, when the wiser cautionary voice of Sir David Steel prevailed over the gung-ho 'let's shoot it out now' approach of Malcolm Bruce. Steel rightly assessed that the longer the Convention existed, the more Labour would seek to avoid a fatal rupture and would be likely to drift to PR. Asserting the repugnance of devolution without PR would also remind Labour of the dangers of division.

But Labour was also interested in appearing to be above partisanship, mainly in strategic furtherance of its thirty-year battle with the SNP, which since the mid 1980s has come to centre around Labour's attempt to claim from the SNP the mantle of being *the* national party of Scotland.

Here, apart from the defensive battle against the SNP on home ground, there was also the offensive strategy to win support in non-traditional areas. Labour's capture in 1987 of such seats as the Western Isles with its unique crofting-based way of life, or middle-class Strathkelvin & Bearsden, demonstrated to many Labour members that the Party could have more than just a class-based appeal. In a Scotland increasingly conscious of a distinctive national identity, that extra dimension could only be given flesh in policies for a Scottish Parliament. Against this background, the Labour Party sailed across the Clyde in March 1990 to Dunoon for a conference that will be remembered by delegates for being interminably rain-sodden as much as for its historic abandonment of First-Past-the-Post.

Though Dewar had been bitterly criticised by Party radicals for being overly cautious, events proved the wisdom of his decision not to try and force a pace faster than his Party would tolerate. For all his fine words of determination to seek agreement in the Convention, Dewar had decided on one simple rule of thumb: 'If it came to a choice between splitting the Party or splitting the Convention, Donald would split the Convention every time,' a colleague said.

The Scottish executive had drawn up a statement for the conference's approval. Unfortunately they made a big mistake. They mentioned the dread words proportional representation, and stated bluntly that in electing a Scottish Parliament 'seats won by any party should reflect the votes cast for that party at Scottish level.' This was overly radical and was duly defeated.

The PR campaigners had, however, seen the problem coming at the pre-conference meetings and made sure that the composited motion on which all their hopes were pinned mentioned only electoral reform and not PR. But the toughest debate came over the criteria for defining the objectives of electoral reform. Words like 'proportional' or 'in proportion' or 'equal', were obviously out. In the end the compositors came up with four criteria. The first was 'A system that fairly rewards parties with representatives broadly equal to the number of votes cast'. It was as loose an approximation to a definition of PR as could be drafted – the words 'broadly equal' having been suggested by the lone delegate from Orkney & Shetland CLP in a flash of inspiration which broke the semantic deadlock.

The other criteria were: 'The system must ensure effective political participation for the sparsely populated areas of Scotland; this system should maintain an element of linkage between representatives and people through constituencies; the electoral system will allow the operation of positive action measures in Labour Party selection procedures.'

Even this ran into trouble. The electricians' union, the EEPTU, suspected, rightly, that it ought to exclude consideration of their preferred electoral system – the Alternative Vote, which is majoritarian and not proportional. They were persuaded to vote for the motion on being told from the platform that it didn't really mean what it said. Thus did the conference, by 372,000 votes to 285,000, muddle its way into history.

The Convention, which various conference speakers warned would be destroyed if Labour did not embrace electoral reform, had achieved its own momentum. The same phenomenon was evident a month later when the STUC annual congress supported electoral reform. General Secretary Campbell Christie and his deputy Bill Speirs have long been self-government radicals, whose activism on the issue of self-government has helped to radicalise the trade unions.

From the women's section of the STUC has come a proposal that the Scottish Parliament's electoral system be so engineered that each constituency should have two MPs, one to be elected from a list of male candidates, and another to be elected from a list of female candidates, thus ensuring that the Scottish Parliament would have 50 per cent male MPs and 50 per cent female MPs. The proposal is strongly opposed by the Liberal Democrats as a form of 'gender apartheid'. There is also more opposition to it within the Labour movement than there appears to be on the surface. Opponents keep quiet because of the abysmal failure of Labour's male-dominated culture to promote women to the degree of prominence which Party policy declares they ought to have in society at large.

Although the 50:50 plan is unlikely to survive in its original form, its radical nature has served to focus attention on other means of ensuring women are able to play a role in a Scottish Parliament. It will certainly have sensible working hours and will not be regularly sitting until the dead of night like the Westminster version.

The reform momentum created at Dunoon did not abate. A reactionary movement to defend First-Past-the-Post did spring up, spear-headed by front-bench MP George Foulkes and Pat Lally, leader of Glasgow District Council. But Lally's declaration that adoption of PR would be the biggest betrayal of the Labour Party since Ramsay MacDonald, and Foulkes' warning that Labour was being held to ransom by pipsqueak Liberals, failed to impress. More influential was the admission by the leader of Strathclyde Regional council, Charles

Gray, that he did not find it healthy that Labour should have won ninety out of 103 seats on the council (87 per cent) with 52 per cent of the vote in May 1990. In March 1991, the Labour conference voted by 517,000 to 125,000 to narrow the electoral reform options down to the Alternative Vote and the Additional Member System.

The same month, the Scottish Liberal Democrat conference reaffirmed rejection of the Alternative Vote, and put forward a variation of their preferred Single Transferable Vote system, called STV-plus, which reduces the size of the multi-member constituencies.

It was only after these votes that the Convention's working party on electoral reform was able to move more swiftly. The Greens had become so fed up with Labour's lumbering manoeuvres that they pulled out of the Convention in November 1990 in protest at the lack of any decision on PR.

Their move was premature, for it was apparent long before then that the Additional Member System, favoured by the Greens, is the only electoral method around which there could be unity in the Convention. By the end of 1991, the working party had honed the options down to variants of AMS, and, even George Foulkes had come to accept AMS as the least bad PR system. The strong likelihood is of some form of AMS being used to elect a Scottish Parliament, and that Labour will be enthusiastic about it.

SOUND-PROOFED COMPARTMENTS?

Though logic suggests the rest of the UK Labour Party may also move towards AMS as the electoral reform debate gathers momentum, experience suggests Scottish political experience is usually regarded as unique and therefore not replicable. Far from Donald Dewar having been instructed by Neil Kinnock on how to handle the issue at every turn, he was left to get on with it and, indeed, reportedly had difficulties persuading Kinnock that there could be serious repercussions from some of the decisions he was taking.

It is often argued that Scottish politics is more consensual than UK politics. This is not entirely true – the gulf of hatred across which Labour and the SNP spit at each other is remarkably deep. But there has been a long tradition of attempting to build alliances across the usual party and social divisions. There have been Conventions in Scotland in 1924, 1926, 1927, 1947, 1948 and 1949. In 1972, the STUC organised a 'Scottish Assembly' on unemployment which was attended by around 1500 people from a range of parties and social organisations. A tripartite body, the Scottish Council for Development and Industry (SCDI), which brings together employers, trade unions and local authorities for genuine debate, remains influential.

Because there are only five million Scots, a degree of intimacy is possible in public life which is not possible south of the border. That intimacy makes understanding of different points of view a lot easier, and consciousness of a much bigger neighbour, England, impels those different points of view to work together. And all the political parties in Scotland play a common game – working to extract as much as possible from that bigger neighbour, something which the UK is having to learn to do better in the context of the EC.

Since senior trade union figures like Gavin Laird of the AEU and John Edmonds of the GMB have followed the Scottish debate closely, as have most Shadow Cabinet members, including the non-Scots, the Scottish experience ought to exert a heavy influence on the UK Labour Party. But the extent to which the UK's different rooms are sound-proofed from each other should not be under-estimated: the extensive experience in Northern Ireland of the STV system advocated by the Liberal Democrats made no impact at all on the Scottish electoral reform debate.

If any noise from the Scottish PR debate leaks through, then what the neighbours ought to hear is that the parameters of the debate were defined by politics rather than by a search for the kind of arithmetical perfectionism to be found in Professor Plant's magisterial survey of electoral reform.

The options thus delineated, choice of system then revolved around two main questions. One was to strike a balance between proportional perfection and simplicity – the Scottish verdict tending towards the simplicity of a system which retains familiar constituencies. The other was to strike a balance between powerful and representative government. With rules to prevent miniscule parties from getting seats, AMS seems to pitch the balance midway. Indeed, if we accept the Nicholas Ridley view of the AMS-elected German government, it can produce very powerful governments.

In Scotland, the Convention's home rule scheme stands much more chance of being welcomed in Orkney and Shetland than the 1979 scheme partly because of PR. If Labour's plans for English regional assemblies get off the ground, then the major headache of drawing acceptable boundaries could well be soothed by PR.

The Scottish experience also provides an antidote to the most commonly expressed reason for being against PR – that it hands too much power to minor parties. There is little doubt, of course, that the Liberal Democrats have had a major influence on the Convention's plans and Labour Party thinking in Scotland. But Donald Dewar has not gone about the country complaining that he has had a gun held at his head, or that Labour has been unable to devise a proper socialist Scottish Parliament. Quite to the contrary, he claimed that Labour's plans commanded the widest support throughout society. Reading between the lines, he was effectively asserting that, as a result of what was an opposition coalition, Labour's policies were strengthened, not weakened.

But because this all stemmed from a crisis, it seems doubtful – in the event of a Labour victory in 1992 – that PR would spread any further than the regional tier of government planned for England and Wales, and the Scottish Parliament. It is more likely to spread downwards into local government than upwards into the House of Commons, where it would be argued that setting up regional systems of government and abolishing the House of Lords was quite enough constitutional legislation for one Parliament.

However, there is a review of parliamentary constituency boundaries due after the 1992 general election which is likely to work in the Conservatives' favour. A tempting tactic for a Labour Government would be to postpone it until after the following general election when it could be combined with an examination of the case for PR in Westminster elections, and of the impact of regional and national assemblies.

If Labour loses the 1992 election, then it would be presented with a massive internal crisis as well as a leadership change. A way forward for the new leadership of John Smith and/or Gordon Brown could lie somewhere between a UK Constitutional Convention to examine the workings of the entire UK government system, and a limited Commission of Inquiry into the electoral system involving the Liberal Democrats. Such an Inquiry would offer a means of making a political counter-attack on the Boundaries Commission review. A Labour conversion to PR would be a convincing base from which to attack the Conservatives as the party clinging to out-dated traditions and attempting to gerrymander themselves into an eternity of government.

Indeed, the hard fact the Labour Party would have to face after a fourth election defeat is that it would be unlikely ever to get into power again except in coalition with the Liberal Democrats or some other party.

One final irony ought to be pointed out. During Labour's PR debate in Scotland, the odd xenophobic voice could be heard arguing against AMS because it was German. Of course, as one of the postwar occupying powers, Britain played a leading role in inventing AMS and Germany's decentralised political system, designed to prevent easy access to a centralised political system by a dictator.

Labour's UK devolution proposals, and the rhetoric used to justify them, sound remarkably like attempts to reinvent what Britain imposed on Germany forty-five years ago. But if a Labour Government does go through with what it says it intends to do, then its actions will be cast in the light of British history, perhaps even as a reinvention of what was disinvented in 1707.

9

WHIGS AND PUNTERS: THE ROLE OF RADICALS IN REACHING REFORM

NINA FISHMAN

When the 1923 general election failed to produce an overall majority in the House of Commons, politicians wondered if First-Past-the-Post could survive. A strong view emerged that the time was ripe for proportional representation: it was both expedient and just. Despite Lloyd George's sabotage of electoral reform as part of the 1918 Representation of the People Act, support for change was serious in all parties.

In May 1924, the Commons debated a Liberal private member's bill to institute PR for general elections. Though the Prime Minister, Ramsay MacDonald, strongly opposed electoral reform, the minority Labour Government allowed a free vote. It was lost on second reading by some 144 votes. Reports agreed that the reason that most Labour MPs had voted against the bill was Asquith's attempt to force the Government's hand. A prescient warning came from the Independent Labour Party veteran, H.N. Brailsford:

> Few reforms can assemble a stronger battery of logical argument than PR. But few make an assault so unwelcome upon our habits or traditions ... PR has the weight of balanced argument behind it. Inevitably our Party (to put it frankly and plainly) must desire the decline and even disappearance of Liberalism. But it would be unworthy to desire or will its decline or defeat by an electoral system which is a trick respectable only by its antiquity.

Brailsford's fears were realised under the second minority Labour Government when, except for principled stalwarts like Philip Snowden and Jimmy Thomas, the bulk of the parliamentary Party defended the status quo for party political reasons. MacDonald's eventual concession, under pressure from the Liberals, of the Alternative Vote came too late to be enacted before the Government's fall in August 1931. Subsequently, conventional Labour wisdom remained caught in a timewarp. It was assumed that First-Past-the-Post was good for Labour, and mere democratic reasons unacceptable for attacking it.

The ghost of Brailsford, however, returned soon enough. The Liberal vote continued to rise throughout the 1960s, and the general election of February 1974 produced the first hung Parliament for nearly half a century. Though the general election in October gave Harold Wilson a narrow (and temporary) majority on less than 40 per cent of the vote, Labour's ascendancy was short-lived.

TRIUMPHALISM AND ABSTRACT INTENTIONS

And indeed the general elections of 1979 and 1983 duly produced large Conservative majorities with little more than 40 per cent of the vote. The haemorrhage of MPs and voters away from Labour after 1979 removed the conditions under which the two-party system could function. First-Past-the-Post now promoted Conservative hegemony.

Towards the end of 1986, as Mrs Thatcher's third election contest loomed, the 'naturally apolitical' British public developed a keen interest, even preoccupation, with the impending contest. The results in three- and four-cornered contests were clearly distorting voters' aggregated intentions. Electoral sums showed that a combination of a divided opposition and First-Past-the-Post was bound to produce a Conservative victory.

And nemesis predictably occurred: a Conservative Government was elected on a 42.3 per cent share of the vote with a majority of 101 in the Commons. Tories who were returned in crucial seats only because the vote against them was divided between Labour and the Alliance nevertheless basked in the general triumphalism which enveloped the Conservative Party. They remained oblivious to the signs that growing numbers of their constituents were seriously disquieted by the manner of their winning.

It is hardly surprising that since 1974 opinion polls have shown marked and steady support for electoral reform. British political culture endows voting for Parliament with special sanctity: people believe that electing the House of Commons is their especial duty, their opportunity to contribute towards the country's future destiny and well-being.

After four successive general elections which have produced distorted results, there is deepening disillusion. Voters increasingly question the solemn democratic ritual in which they have always played their allotted part. The 'Thatcher generation' has grown to political maturity in this time. They have witnessed only 'abnormal' general elections. They vote for the first time with no great confidence that their votes will count.

Nevertheless, the undeniable popular majority for a fairer voting system remains hypothetical and untested. It is one thing for millions of voters to agree with the principle of proportional representation, and it is quite another for their abstract intentions to be mobilised behind an assault on First-Past-the-Post. Around Westminster, the majority view is that while electoral reform may be worthy, it will ultimately prove unworkable. Many seasoned observers believe the prospect of electoral reform is dependent on a succession of hung Parliaments.

There is certainly a vast array of vested interests ranged against electoral reform. Any change in the voting system would have uncomfortable consequences for MPs and their retinues. Government and Opposition alike would have to change the habits of a lifetime. The perpetual perk of approximately 535 safe seats would disappear, and general elections would again become genuinely uncertain contests. Politicians would be constrained to take 'the punters' a great deal more seriously.

THE TWO HALVES OF WHIGGERY

There is no mystery shrouding both Front Benches' devotion to the *status quo*. It is part of their role under the unwritten constitution to damp down the dangerous enthusiasms of reformers who expend their energy and emotion in campaigning. A strong reflex against excessive zeal was embedded in the British political establishment's psyche during the English Civil War, and informed their Whig outlook. Whiggery holds that, whatever their political hue, radicals who believe in causes may be virtuous, but are likely to be disappointed: it is preferable to be stoic than to pin one's hopes on an ultimately hopeless crusade.

I am conscious of the risk of alienating contemporary readers by using 'Whig' without quotation marks or an implied sneer. I have revived the term because it more accurately describes this vital part of British political culture than other available alternatives, such as 'reformist', 'mandarin', or 'liberal'. Though significant Whig grandees adhered to the Liberal Party as it emerged in the 1850s, Whiggery was also firmly anchored in the Tory Party by Disraeli.

The political establishment and the press gradually stopped using 'Whig' approvingly to describe contemporary politicians' behaviour towards the end of the nineteenth century. The evolution of a substantial democratic political culture then made Whiggery appear an anachronism. Its essential principles were subsumed under the general rubric of 'responsible' governance and the ethics of 'stewardship'. However, many Whig reflexes survive and continue to provide guides to action for all sections of the political establishment.

When Mrs Thatcher's radical principles finally proved an embarrassment and an electoral liability, she was replaced by the most substantial Whig of the three contenders. Mr Major's celebrated greyness reflects the hallowed Whig perspective: he is content to do nothing very much, very well, for most of the time.

During his tenure of the Labour leadership, Neil Kinnock has presided over the Parliamentary Labour Party's enforced conversion to thorough-going Whiggery. He entered the House imbued with the rugged radicalism of South Wales political culture. Nevertheless, faced with the prospect of permanent opposition, he has proved as adept at Whiggery as his revered Tredegar predecessor Aneurin Bevan could be when the occasion demanded. The Shadow Cabinet now looks and behaves like a potential government, in a Whiggish fashion. Kinnock has been amply rewarded for his efforts by Labour's rise in the opinion polls.

Scepticism about opinion poll support for proportional representation being transformed into actual reform is informed by a shrewd appreciation of the Whiggish prejudice against serious change held by the political establishment. The cynical aphorism, which has become a cliché because of its predictive accuracy, is that vested interests will prevail and politicians will continue to sleep easy in their beds. It is true that Labour Party managers have encouraged the Plant

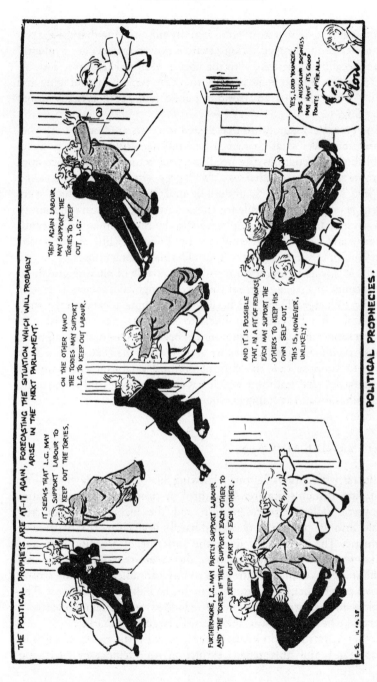

POLITICAL PROPHECIES.

Low, *Evening Standard*, 11 October 1928. Courtesy of the Electoral Reform Society Library.

Commission to deliberate in good faith (while ensuring that the Party's bets are carefully hedged). Conservative power-brokers are evidently willing to allow flirtations with the idea of electoral reform to indulge intellectuals and keen believers: but they also remain discouraging and evasive when there is any serious public talk about actually doing something.

However, the assumption that vested interests are bound to prevail ignores the other vital characteristic of Whiggery: that the political establishment recognises the need to enact reform when it becomes unavoidable. It was both halves of Whiggery – its distaste for crusading zeal *and* its willingness to undertake practical reform – which were held to be mainly responsible for the country's comparative immunity from violent and disruptive upheavals in the revolutionary nineteenth century, and which were emulated by European liberal politicians from Guizot to Cavour and the South German ruling houses.

Both Major and Kinnock are still well capable of altering course to take account of a strong current running through civil society in favour of radical change. They will hardly do anything to encourage such change, but they are equally unlikely to try sabotage or suppression to evade reform when public opinion has been mobilised in its support. Whigs haven't resorted to that sort of thing since the 1660s. There is no reason to suppose that the current political establishment wants to rupture a political tradition which has been so successful in ensuring social cohesion and avoiding mayhem.

WHIGS AND RADICALS

In the early twentieth century, leftwing historians made the telling point that Britain's apparently unbroken procession towards more democratic political representation and the incorporation of 'the people' into the political process had hardly been either trouble-free or automatic. The sacrifice of lives, the suffering of working men and women for their political principles, the severe repression of radicals by the state, governments' attempts to buy off radicals, and the strong opposition of much of the establishment, had all held up reform. The Panglossian picture of inevitable progress in Britain towards a Benthamite better place was, they argued, largely mythical.

However, in the mid twentieth century, with the rise of fascism in Europe and the threatened extinction of democracy, leftwing historians and politicians who had previously spurned Whiggery began to see its advantages. They acknowledged that Britain's road to reform had indeed been bumpy, but nevertheless recognised that there was something to be said in favour of a 'ruling class' which acquiesced in the reform of the *status quo* when it could not be avoided. They also became interested in the role which radicals had played.

It is not surprising that both radicals and establishment figures should arrive at a more balanced view of Whiggery. In the long and painful build-up to fighting another total war in 1939, British political activists had to be certain what they were fighting *for*. No one in power or on its fringes wanted another war. The deep popular reaction against war which occurred after November 1918 was prolonged. Radicals needed to be certain that the differences separating Britain from the Third Reich were indeed profound, and that this peculiar British political culture with its liberty and Whiggery was worth defending.

It is, though, still true that the British political process will only yield reform when all sections take their roles seriously. The significant political reforms enacted in Britain during the nineteenth and early twentieth centuries are evidence of the vision and determination of crusading British radicals. They were undeterred by adverse fortune or the apparently impregnable stonewall of an unbending establishment. Consequently, they were able to take advantage of favourable circumstance, when it appeared, to effect significant breaches in the establishment's defences. Wellington, Grey, Disraeli, and Salisbury all foisted substantial and ultimately subversive democratic reforms on unwilling Parliaments because they were able to paint the unpalatable consequences of not reforming so vividly. They had earnest radicals at their heels agitating for far-reaching structural reforms. The unwilling House of Commons acquiesced in enacting milder reforms as the lesser of two evils.

RADICALS AND PUNTERS

The key to gaining electoral reform lies on the radical side of British politics. It requires the active intervention of political activists to give popular frustrations, grievances and problems a political shape. Electoral reform is no exception. Voting systems and legislative arrangements have never sprung Minerva-like in owl suits from the collective head of 'the people'. That myth is part of the political culture of 'the people' begun in France in 1789 and revived after the Russian Revolution of 1917. Like all persistent myths, it has some truth – in this case teaching the lesson of *connectedness*, the need for political activists to heed what is going on in the real world of civil society. But the job of positively encouraging and nurturing political reform belongs to a minority, the radical section of political activism.

A model case may be the campaign waged by liberals and radicals in the 1820s to remove the restrictions on trade union organisation. The campaign was orchestrated by Francis Place, the London tailor, who kept a foot in both camps – the leftish wing of the political establishment and the 'common people' who were organising trade unions illegally. By acting as intermediary between civil society and the state, Place stage-managed a major reform which was to have significant consequences for the future course of Britain.[1]

The part of radicals in the British political process remains far from easy. They are comparatively isolated for most of a reform's gestation period. Though the need for reform is clear to those with radical vision, the attention and interest of mainstream politicians and the public are usually diverted by more 'pressing' issues which arise from the current cut-and-thrust of politics. There is always a raft of truly compelling reasons for delaying political change – a miners' strike, rising unemployment, and the prospect of a pernicious war were contingencies present in 1923-24 to divert attention from the claims of proportional representation. In a period of comparative foreign and economic calm, when radicals succeed in engaging popular and establishment attention, there are still the legendary vested interests and the inertia of the *status quo* to overcome.

Margaret Thatcher made a great mistake in enacting a substantial reform, the poll tax, without first ensuring that her radical political supporters had forged a close partnership with the substantial sections of society whose support is crucial. Despite her famous contempt for 'consensus politics', she shared its assumption that a law passed by Parliament would automatically be obeyed by the law-abiding British public. Trained as a chemist rather than as a political historian, the lessons of nineteenth-century reforms were lost on her. She failed to realise that the participation of radical political activists is essential to secure popular enthusiasm for and adherence to serious change. She thought that a British government once elected could govern without reference to civil society. That assumption holds true *most* of the time.

The clear exception occurs when a government is determined upon substantial economic or political reform. Then the Whiggish prejudices against change both inside the political establishment and within civil society act powerfully to reinforce the *status quo*.

The moderation in popular political culture has developed in emulation of the establishment's Whiggery. But alongside a prejudice against extreme or even radical change, there is a pragmatic reformist side to popular political culture which responds to important 'grievances' which need 'redress'. In addition, there is a strong vein of stern moralism, originating in non-conformism, which has always been effective in enlisting collective support for radical action to right outrageous injustice. There has always been support for reform coming from crucial sections of British society *when the case for practical change has been seriously made*.

In 1974, the opportunity to gain electoral reform was lost because radicals declined to engage with the British public's actual state of mind, which was then inclined towards pragmatic reform. With the combination of a hung Parliament, a minority Labour government and a shaken (and shaky) political establishment, substantial sections of society might have supported proportional representation if they had been given the chance.

It is a supreme irony, then, that it was not the political establishment who were primarily responsible for prolonging First-Past-the-Post. It was not the dead wood of backbench MPs who would lose their seats through proportional representation, nor the conservative bias in the House of Commons against reforming itself. These obstructive factors undoubtedly existed, but the vested interests were doing no more or less than they had done during the nineteenth century, when their obstructiveness had failed to hold back the tide of reform. Most British radicals were unwilling to take any piecemeal, practical reform seriously. The Liberal Party and its activists were sadly isolated in their insistence that electoral reform was a just and worthy aim. One section of leftwing radicals cried that nothing less than revolution would do. They opted out of any involvement with popular political culture and the mainstream British political process. From their perspective, electoral reform was just another trick: proportional representation would perpetuate the fatal illusion that voting could change things. They couldn't conceive of the possibility that proportional representation might be worth fighting for because it would bring about a greater connectedness between the political establishment and voters. They were posturing without intent.

FORGING NEW CONNECTIONS

Radicals' disillusionment with Whiggery had become acute in the 1960s, and this disillusionment bred a lack of understanding of their role in precipitating change in our Whiggish political system. There were healthy reasons at the time for reacting against Whiggery, which had become a stifling orthodoxy. The lively, flexible side of Britain's political culture had been stultified by the sheer weight of triumphalism at winning the war. Not just the flag-waving right, but the liberal-left establishment never tired of recalling the miraculous national characteristics of political moderation and gradual, piecemeal reform – Britain's delivery of the the whole continent from the forces of darkness and fascism in the 1939-45 war was a certain sign of the potency of parliamentary democracy.

While these sentiments were accurate, they became increasingly complacent. The political establishment had actually stopped thinking about politics. They were absolutely certain that the virtues of British parliamentary democracy were an eternal verity which would be amply rewarded on the day when nations and peoples were finally called to account. Their overweening smugness alienated 1960s adolescents. Radicals like myself couldn't stomach the complacent assumption that British politicians had always been wise, prudently adaptable, and far-sighted in their provision for future changes. It was this stuffy self-satisfaction which David Frost and his *enfants terribles* attacked on *That Was The Week That Was*, and which *Private Eye* dented so tellingly.

And besides, radicals' reactions were only more extreme manifestations of the growing popular disaffection with 'them', the political establishment. British citizens had become genuinely impatient with the last residues of nineteenth-century class hierarchies. The levelling process which had been fermenting away within civil society since 1939 had not been adequately reflected either inside the political establishment or in the connections between Westminster and the people. Moreover, British political culture, with the the strong presumption of due political process, assisted this newly self-confident citizenry in developing their grievance against 'them'. In the 1960s, people still had a rough notion of how a Britain governed by real representatives ought to be functioning.

If notions of due process had been repressed and almost forgotten by politicians themselves during the era of 'consensus' politics (see the appendix on 'Electoral Reform in Historical Perspective'), the 'punters' still thought they were entitled to democratic government. They were fed up with the current lot of politicians who were *not* reflecting their own priorities and concerns. Sometime in the mid 1970s, Hugh Trevor Roper (now Lord Dacre) remarked with the majestic understatement so typical of Whiggery that the British establishment had succumbed in the 1960s to the relentless drip, drip, drip of satire. Things, he gloomily opined, would never be the same again.

After over a decade, it is difficult to remember the feelings of vulnerability and unease which pervaded the corridors of power then. Everyone agreed that something was bound to happen. When the National Union of Mineworkers precipitated the downfall of a Tory government, the air of expectation increased. Socialists inside and outside the Labour Party expected that whatever happened next, it would move Britain further in their direction. But monetarist radicals within the Conservative Party were also beginning to flex their muscles.

Feelings of insecurity inside the political establishment were justified. There was a disenchantment with leaders who behaved as if Britain was still bestride the world, and were evidently oblivious to the real problems at home. There was a quiet but acute apprehension that the political process connecting politicians to the people had failed.

In this situation, the abolition of First-Past-the-Post was potentially a crucial, substantial and far-reaching political reform. The electoral reform of the House of Commons would make the political establishment truly insecure for at least a generation: in order to assure their own places, they would have to forge new links with the people they were supposed to be representing. Like the great nineteenth-century reforms of the suffrage, proportional representation would mark an advance for democracy.

But because radicals were unwilling to embark on the road to electoral reform, the opportunity thrown up by the circumstance in 1974 of a hung Parliament was missed. The case for proportional representation went by default. The political impasse was resolved by the Wilson/Callaghan Governments through fudge, and disillusion with Labour's radical credentials increased. The desire for political

THE MASQUERADE

DOESN'T IT MAKE A LOVELY SPREAD?

THE JACKDAW WITH THE PEACOCK'S TAIL

(Under a just system of Proportional Representation the Government's inflated majority of nearly 250 would be reduced, on the number of votes cast, to 48.)

Holland, 1935. Courtesy of the Electoral Reform Society Library.

change within civil society deepened, and, although it sat ill with the Tory grandees, Mrs Thatcher's crusading radicalism was undeniably popular. Her arguments were at first hearing persuasive, and people were prepared to let her have a go. The hopes aroused and then disappointed by Margaret Thatcher have produced a favourable fall-out for radicals. Contrary to many fatalist predictions, voting for Thatcher was not a sign of a popular conversion to her atomist, atavist worldview. The pragmatic moderation of British political culture has emerged dominant.

The portents are now extremely good for the cause of electoral reform. Public opinion is favourable and waiting to be mobilised. The political establishment is currently showing its grey stony face, but is increasingly inclined by the messages coming from civil society to cultivate an open mind. All parts of the establishment are discreetly, but diligently, investigating alternative electoral systems. They want to discover which ones would involve the minimum change to their own habits.

There is nothing inherent in popular political culture which inhibits public support from being mobilised behind a campaign for proportional representation. There is a clear critical mass of British citizens who are, if not already converted, open to persuasion. If a compelling case is made, they will agree that change should occur and will consequently support it.

The unanswered question is whether radicals will take advantage of this favourable opportunity to promote PR. Have they learned how to be practical and pilot this reformist political objective through all the obstacles presented by the forces of the *status quo*?

Unless radicals set their sights on achieving a limited and tangible goal, the mood in favour of change will again be dissipated. With an abundance of circumstances favouring electoral reform, it would be folly to throw away such good fortune.

NOTE

1 Place's Fabian biographer, Graham Wallas, rescued him from an unjustified obscurity with his *The Life of Francis Place*, first published in 1898 (Allen & Unwin, London; revised edition, 1918).

APPENDIX: ELECTORAL REFORM IN HISTORICAL PERSPECTIVE

One of the enduring myths of European political culture is that electing parliamentarians has always been the sacred heart of the nation-state, providing the lifeblood of democracy, keeping the body politic in good health. Political historians, notably Guizot, Macaulay and Froude, described a smooth, stately processing of consultative democracy throughout Europe from the twelfth century when kings and queens founding strong states had extended pre-Roman tribal meetings to include gentry and merchants. These historians marshalled convincing evidence to fill out a fascinating picture of the continuous development of representative institutions.

In fact, this carefully crafted myth of Saxons, Franks, Lombards, Visigoths, Vandals and Gauls electing their respective *folksmoot* representatives was an attempt to neutralise the inflammatory ideas of popular democracy powerfully stimulated by the French Revolution. The picture of a long inheritance of benevolent representative institutions gave the European political establishments a comforting perspective on difficult, discontinuous times and the often violent conflicts which they had just lived through.

The incorporation of a democratic underpinning to European states was painful and protracted. The establishment's acquiescence in democratic ways began haltingly and grudgingly in France and Britain in the 1830s. Moreover, it was only during the last quarter of the nineteenth century that most European political establishments finally accepted elections as the only reliable way of integrating 'the masses' into politics.

It would be foolish to pretend, of course, that the political establishment was the sole beneficiary from this new system of representative government of the late 1800s. Elections based on universal or wide manhood suffrage proved popular with the people, and were a watershed in the development of liberal democratic pluralism.

In the 1990s, supporters of proportional representation argue that citizens in a democracy are entitled to votes of equal value, and that the abolition of First-Past-the-Post would continue a widening of the base of the British body politic begun a century and a half ago. By contrast, many of the early supporters of proportional representation in Britain viewed it as a corrective to the dangerous democratic currents being released by the enlargement of the suffrage begun in 1832 and continued by Disraeli in 1867. In 1884-85, some of the founders of the Proportional Representation Society (forerunner of the present Electoral Reform Society) believed that PR provided a means of ensuring the continued representation of the minority interests of property.[1] For a while, Conservative leaders considered that PR might provide a counterbalance to curb the untried impulses of the large reservoir of new voters: Arthur Balfour was a committed supporter, and his uncle Salisbury seriously considered promoting a new proportional voting system.

It soon became evident, however, that the men who had gained the vote (and the women who had not) had been successfully incorporated by the political establishment into the new mass political culture. They were caught up in the new set of events and ritualised conflicts surrounding elections and the enlarged political parties which fought them. New forms of communication, education and entertainment appeared: the growth of a popular political press, pamphleteering, meetings and debates in every town and village. The new connection between the political establishment and civil society was a great success and there was no need to upset Westminster vested interests by introducing comprehensive electoral reform.

The perception of voting as the cornerstone of popular democracy was shared by many socialist activists. When the Belgian Assembly refused to agree any enlargement of the franchise, after almost three years of examining different schemes, the Socialist Party called a general strike in 1893. The strike attracted a level of support frightening to the establishment, and after seven days, the Assembly conceded very much more than had previously been contemplated, enlarging the electorate from 137,000 to 1,381,000.[2]

This spectacular success was much discussed inside the Socialist International. Pragmatic socialists argued that the Belgian achievement should be emulated elsewhere. More revolutionary socialists wanted to use the general strike to overthrow the existing state: they were contemptuous of the value of voting. In the early years of the twentieth century, there was a protracted dispute inside the German socialist party (SPD) about whether to fight seriously, with a general strike if necessary, for a universal franchise in Prussia (which maintained a notoriously restricted male suffrage). The conflict between 'reformists' and 'revolutionaries', however, was papered over, and the Diet remained a bastion of Junker privilege.

In the southern German states, on the other hand, where liberal political establishments had early conceded broad-based male suffrage, the SPD enjoyed both political power and influence. There was a strong undercurrent of contempt inside the SPD towards the compromises and reforms of the southern German socialist deputies. It reflected an ambivalence about voting and elections which had important consequences for the fate of the Weimar Republic.

In Britain, the political establishment felt that the results of the 1884 extension of the franchise proved the efficacy of citizenship as a means of incorporating the masses into the body politic. The Tories believed that they had everything to gain by initiating the working man into politics. While property-ownership instilled a sense of proprietorship and provided a stake in the system, vote-owning was seen as means of accomplishing the same end in the wider civic arena.

Both trade unions and socialists were quick to recognise the potential of the extended suffrage. The cause of independent 'Labour' representation was greatly assisted by local Liberal associations' refusal to adopt working-class candidates, despite the pleadings of Westminster Liberal whips. By the turn of the twentieth century, the Labour Party had become a focus for working-class aspirations, and an avenue by which ambitious independent men without means, like Ramsay Macdonald, could make their political way.

By the 1890s, there was a strong consensus among radicals in favour of further democratic reform. Socialists in the Independent Labour Party, the Fabian Society and trade union activists were committed to greater political democracy. The radical parts of the political establishment (from the Unionist Joseph Chamberlain to the Liberals Labouchere and Morley) were minded to defuse the intensifying economic struggle through some form of political settlement. There was increasing interest among Liberal intellectuals in the collectivist ideas of continental and Fabian socialism.

Some radicals, trade union leaders and many Independent Labour

Party activists (including Keir Hardie) supported proportional representation. They recognised that in three-cornered contests the infant Labour Party would usually be the loser. In Belgium, where since 1893 three-cornered contests had reinforced the previous domination of the Catholic Party over the Liberals and Socialists, proportional representation in constituencies had been enacted in 1899.[3] In Britain, Labour activists looked to PR to provide them with a springboard for substantial representation in the Commons and real power and influence in politics.

The 1890s and early years of the twentieth century were characterised by civil society's growing self-confidence in questioning the decisions of the political establishment. The culture of responsible citizenship began to be preached by adult educationalists, and popular textbooks were written about how true Britons had always been both subject and citizen.

If war had not intervened, further democratic reform in Britain would probably have been enacted by whatever government had succeeded Asquith, who had been opposed to further political 'experiments'. The previous twenty-five years had seen an unprecedented upsurge in popular interest in politics in all European countries, including Britain. The reasons are complex and interconnected: increasing industrialisation, intensifying class struggle, growing trade union membership, greater literacy and new forms of collective voluntary activity. The more prudent and energetic parts of the political establishment sensed that the time was ripe for a fresh round of democratising to put more flesh on the bones connecting the establishment and civil society.

The crucible of total war had a dramatic levelling effect on all European nation-states, precipitating a more democratic political culture. It was palpably clear that every citizen should sacrifice equally and be rewarded accordingly. To ensure that war production continued to flow, the socialist and trade union movements were brought into the heart of the political establishment.

'Consensus politics' in Europe, involving the whole nation from factory floor to the surviving institutions of the *ancien régime*, dates from 1914. In practice, 'consensus' meant civil society agreeing to curtail its freedoms and acquiescing in the contraction of due political process. The methods adopted to fight the war were centralising and corporatist. The connections between the political establishment and civil society became purely functional and practical. Politicians had no time to purvey, foster and develop political culture. They abjured domestic political conflict and got on with the pressing business of war production, recruiting soldiers, organising propaganda, and dealing with industrial unrest.

In Britain, Labour's political culture was decisively shaped by the moment of its assumption of a share of serious political power. The corporatist organisation of civil society for a single collective aim convinced Labour activists and intellectuals alike that Britain was ripe for socialism. Most of them failed to remake their old connections with the culture of democratic reform, and were indifferent to the problem of rebuilding a robust democratic politics.

The Labour leadership wanted to cement their Party's claim to governance. They wanted to wield power. Because of the Liberals' demoralisation and divisions after 1918, Labour easily won large numbers of new seats under First-Past-the-Post. In the wake of the Liberals' collapse, the Labour leadership became first increasingly sceptical and then downright hostile towards proportional representation. They were unconcerned with the needs and rights of civil society and alive only to their own opportunity to claim the Liberals' empty places.

The left wing of the Labour Party were antagonistic to PR for different, though equally self-serving, reasons. They continued to be preoccupied with the centralising experiments of the wartime emergency, seeing them as providing the foundations of a non-capitalist economic order. In the wake of the Russian Revolution, they were increasingly drawn to the revolutionary side of socialist politics which denied that elections were anything more than a 'bourgeois charade'. The unseemly combination of the leadership's realpolitik and the left's 'revolutionary' inclinations meant that there was no widespread support for PR inside the Parliamentary Labour Party throughout the interwar period.

Politicians became accustomed to managing civil society, and, not surprisingly, the conventions and habits associated with fighting total war persisted throughout the 1920s and 1930s. With hindsight, historians are increasingly viewing the period from 1914 to 1945 as unitary – one prolonged total war, punctuated in the middle by an uneasy armed truce. From its inception in the wartime emergency, 'consensus' actually meant the disengagement of the political establishment from the due political processes connecting it to civil society. Ironically, by the 1950s, it was assumed that 'consensus politics' must signify full and active consent from all parts of civil society to a course of action upon which the political establishment had agreed.

As far as civil society was concerned, however, the voluntary surrender of political rights and freedom in 1914 had never been intended as permanent. By the 1970s, 'ordinary people' had become thoroughly disaffected by the false assumption of 'consensus politics'. They knew they had not given their active consent to the perpetual surrender of their political rights.

The trouble was that citizens in civil society were without a champion. Those who should have been arguing for a renewal of representative democracy were either indifferent or downright contemptuous towards 'feeble' solutions like electoral reform.

NOTES

1 The Society has finally received a full historical analysis in Jenifer Hart, *Proportional Representation: Critics of the British Electoral System 1820-1945*, Oxford University Press, Oxford 1992.
2 See E.H. Kossmann, *The Low Countries, 1780-1940*, Oxford University Press, Oxford 1978.
3 *Ibid.*

10

VOTERS, QUOTAS, AND WOMEN IN THE HOUSE

ANNA KRUTHOFFER

Britain's First-Past-the-Post voting system allowed one woman Prime Minister to make history, but gave us a Parliament where only six per cent of MPs were women when she left office. And as Geraldine Ferraro, the first woman US vice-Presidential candidate, quipped – the point is to have 'less of us making history and more of us making policy'.

Women face discrimination in every area of their lives and perhaps no one should expect the political arena to be different. Lynda Chalker spent many years as 'one woman alongside a whole lot of men' as a statistician in market research for Unilever, Shell Mex, Barclays Bank and BP; yet she found 'that in the political sphere it was more difficult than it had ever been in business.'[1] But unless women can take hold of political power, can other areas of their lives be improved?

A lack of economic independence and the combination of domestic and work responsibilities militate against women's participation even in local politics, let alone national government. Westminster working hours, the lack of childcare facilities and the male 'club' atmosphere are additional factors now generally acknowledged as reasons why women have not flocked to the House of Commons, although they make up 52 per cent of the population.

But, as anyone who has ever organised a political event will know, simply laying on crèche facilities does not result in huge numbers of women attending. More fundamental and institutional structures within our political system have to be challenged. These include the way that both parties and Parliament operate, but the key to these changes is the voting system.

COMING FORWARD ...

First-Past-the-Post works systematically against women, both as voters and as candidates. It stands in the way of any attempts to redress the gender balance in Parliament or to allow effective representation of women's views in the decision-making processes. A look at the history (and so at the limited progress) of women in British political life suggests that even if, on its own, the electoral system cannot be 'blamed' for the fact that Britain has one of the lowest numbers of women in Europe in its Parliament, unless the electoral system is changed other positive action to encourage women to enter politics cannot succeed. The 1990 report of the Hansard Society *Women at the Top* goes so far as to state:

> The First-Past-the-Post electoral system is likely to be one of the main reasons for the low representation of women in the House of Commons. It may also be among the main reasons why the United States, despite its highly active women's movement, has such low representation of women in Congress.

Women have been active in British political parties since the 1880s. Nearly half the Conservatives' Primrose League were women, the Women's Liberal Federation was established in 1887, and Labour followed in 1906 with the Women's Labour League. Women ratepayers had, to a limited extent, emerged in local politics since the Municipal Franchise Act of 1869, participating in elections to parish, district and county councils. Many were also elected to other bodies such as those governing education or welfare bodies: by 1900, 1147 women had been elected to boards of Poor Law Guardians.[2]

The proportion of women in local government is still higher than at national level. Around a quarter of councillors are women, although there is marked regional variation: in Wales, for example, only around one in twenty councillors is female, whereas in the south east women make up a third of some councils. On occasion some council chambers – such as Brighton, Norfolk and Oxford – have been more than half filled by women. There have been a number of women council leaders, some of whom, such as Lady Porter in Westminster, have held positions that have taken on national significance.

However, women's progression into national politics has not been so straightforward. Women have always had to fight for their rights, and quite often the women who have done the fighting have not made it into the history books. Sylvia Pankhurst said of Margaret Bondfield, one of the early women MPs, that it was 'a curious fact that the women who secured political office when the citizenship of women was achieved had none of them taken a prominent part in the struggle for the vote'. In a marked contrast to Margaret Thatcher, Mary Robinson expressly recognised the role of women in securing her election as President of the Irish Republic: 'As a woman, I want women who have felt themselves outside history to be written back into history, in the words of Eavan Boland, "Finding a voice where they found a vision".'[3]

The first woman MP in Britain was elected at the 1918 general election – when women (over the age of 30) were first able to vote – but as a member of Sinn Fein, Constance Markievicz never took up her seat. The first woman to take her seat in the Commons was Nancy Astor in 1919.

In 1928 women were given the vote on an equal basis with men and from then on have formed the majority of the electorate. In 1929 the additional six million female voters contributed to the election of fourteen women. However, it was not until the 1987 general election that women actually became the majority of voters, and there is still a long way to go before women are the majority of those elected!

The forty-four women who sat in the 1987-92 Parliament were a larger contingent than ever before, but this figure should not be regarded as part of a continuous trend of gradual increase since 1928. Only 139 women have *ever* sat in the House of Commons, and between 1945 and 1991 the number has fluctuated between a low of seventeen in 1951 and the pre-1987 high of twenty-nine, which was achieved in 1964.

It has never been a lack of enthusiasm for politics that has resulted in such low numbers of women being elected. Where they have been allowed to, women have become involved. And from a look at the numbers of women taking part in general election contests, it can been seen that the problem is not one of 'women not coming forward'. The number of female candidates has risen steadily to 329, or 14 per cent, at the 1987 election.

To see why the present system fails female candidates, one must look not just at elections, but at the way candidates are picked. Women who wish to be considered by the local party selection committee have to contend with the selectors' stereotyped and sexist assumptions about what constitutes an 'electable' candidate. Lesley Abdela's *Women with X Appeal* is based on interviews with women who have fought parliamentary seats and highlights the obstacles they have faced. Many refer to the selection procedures followed by the main political parties.

Tory hopeful Doreen Miller recalls being asked questions at her selection interview which would never have been put to a male candidate: 'Don't you think it's rather presumptuous for you to think we should select you for the House of Commons when you haven't even stood for the local council?' Alliance hopeful Linda Siegle complains that women are invisible to the parties, citing an exchange with a former Liberal chairman when she complained of a lack of women on the Alliance general election campaign committee in 1987. She was told, 'We really are very aware of that problem ... but there simply were no suitable women.' Linda replied, 'You wouldn't know a suitable woman if you fell over one in the street.'

Another Conservative, Angela Browning, summarised a general frustration – 'The stereotype of the male candidate in the pin-striped suit with two little children and a very nice wife is still uppermost in people's minds – even though we have a woman prime minister.'

Angela Hooper, along with Janet Young, campaigned in the early 1980s to have more women selected as candidates by the Conservative Party.[4] They developed tactics to challenge the criteria used by selection committees: 'One of the key things is to have a choice of more than one woman, so that one woman can't be rejected because she's got the wrong shoes. One woman wore Hush Puppies in an interview for an urban seat! And another wore a black suit – no way!'

... AND GETTING ELECTED?

Even if a woman does get selected by her party, it is often for an unwinnable seat. The more likely the party thinks it is to win a seat, the more likely it is to fall back on the 'traditional' candidate to fight it. Successive population and boundary changes have resulted in more and more seats that are 'safe' for one or other of the main parties.

This probably contributes to the widening gap between the number of women *selected* and the number *elected*. The number of women selected has increased from 5.1 per cent of candidates in 1964 to 14.2 per cent in 1987, but the number elected has increased only from 4.6 per cent of MPs to 6.3 per cent. Part of the difficulty arises because any attempt to increase the number of women MPs has to mean selecting them for safe seats, and so throwing out sitting (probably white, middle-aged) male MPs. Understandably, the parties shy away from this. Pippa Norris and Joni Lovenduski, in their submission to the Labour Party's commission on electoral systems, argued that 'greater proportionality increases legislative turnover', and that if seats change hands more often there could be greater access for women and other less 'traditional' candidates.

The establishment of a new party can provide opportunities for women because the problem of de-selecting sitting MPs is sidestepped. The SDP/Liberal Alliance stood 105 women in 1987, representing a much higher percentage of their candidates than either Labour, who stood 92 women, or the Conservatives, who put only 46 women forward. It has been argued that a proportional system would more readily allow for the formation of new parties. It is certainly true that if the electoral system does not enable fair representation of parties, positive initiatives even in parties with as wide support as the 22.6 per cent gained by the Alliance in 1987 will not necessarily translate into more women MPs.

The table and figure compare the number of women in the lower houses of parliaments in different countries. It is more than coincidence that the countries which do not use a form of PR have among the lowest numbers of women. Occasionally, higher than usual numbers of women are elected under First-Past-the-Post, but this tends to be the result of an unexpected landslide for one particular party, leading to the election of women for seats the party did not originally expect to win. The percentages shown for Canada and New Zealand are examples of this, as was the surprisingly high number of women elected at the time of the 1945 Labour victory in Britain.

A large number of those countries where there are high levels of women in parliament use some type of party list system. However, suggestions that party lists could be used to improve the situation in Britain are generally not welcomed for two main reasons – that the list system gives too much power to parties; and that the link between the MP and constituency is broken. So simple list systems have been almost

Table 10.1   Women in Elected Office in Developed Democracies, 1991

Country	%	Year	Index of Prop.	Ballot List
Proportional party lists				
Finland	38	1991	89	Reg. List
Sweden	38	1988	97	Reg. List
Norway	36	1989	91	Reg. List
Denmark	33	1990	95	Reg. List
Iceland	24	1991	96	Reg. List
Austria	22	1990	99	Reg. List
Netherlands	21	1989	96	Nat. List
Germany	20	1990	99	AMS
Switzerland	16	1991	96	Reg. List
Spain	15	1989	87	Reg. List
Luxembourg	13	1989	91	Reg. List
Italy	13	1987	95	Reg. List
Israel	7	1990	93	Nat. List
Portugal	8	1987	91	Reg. List
Belgium	8	1987	92	Reg. List
Greece	5	1990	88	Reg. List
Plurality systems				
New Zealand	16	1990	88	FPTP
Canada	13	1988	86	FPTP
United States	6	1990	94	FPTP
UK	6	1987	79	FPTP
Majority				
Australia	7	1990	87	AV
France	6	1988	81	Second Ballot
STV systems				
Ireland	8	1989	95	STV
Malta	3	1987	100	STV

Note: the Index of Proportionality is calculated as the sum of the differences between each party's share of seats and its share of votes, divided by two and subtracted from 1090.

Source: *Distribution of Seats Between Men and Women in National Assemblies*, June 1991 (CIDP, Geneva 1987).

Figure 10.1 Percentage of Women in the Lower House, 1991

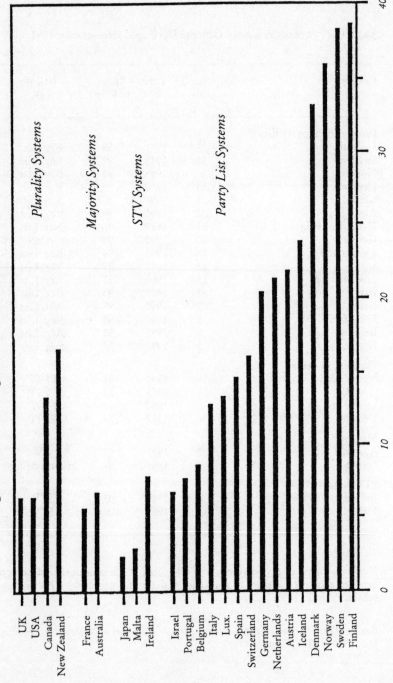

totally disregarded in recent discussions of alternative electoral systems – for example for a Scottish Assembly or as part of Labour's working party on electoral systems.

The hybrid Additional Member System used in Germany has, however, been put forward as a serious possibility for Britain. Part of the argument in its favour has been gender balance: regional lists could be used to 'top up' the gender quotas in Parliament resulting from constituency elections. This reflects the German experience: women MPs made up just over 20 per cent of the total in the German Bundestag in 1990, although they won only 12 per cent of constituency seats. 28 per cent of those elected from the lists were women.

Any system which creates two different types of MP raises a number of questions. Are both types regarded as equal? Does the constituency MP have greater legitimacy than a 'best loser' elected from the list? And is it fair that the list MPs have time to develop a higher profile, especially in a pre-election period, than the local MP whose time and energy are taken up with constituency duties? And for the female candidate herself, would anyone want to be imposed as MP for a regional electorate which had already rejected her at the constituency level?

How the constituency MPs under AMS are elected is important. In Germany First-Past-the-Post is used; the Alternative Vote is proposed by the Scottish National Party for an AMS-elected independent Scottish Parliament: in both, the problem of remains of de-selecting sitting male MPs from single-member seats.

The belief that this system will produce more women MPs relies on the assumption that the central or regional party organisation would use its increased power to select women for the party list. But could this be guaranteed? And should a particular electoral system be chosen because national parties are seen, at the moment, to be more in favour of women than local parties? Are local party members happy to surrender control of candidate choice in this way, especially when the national party not only uses its power to influence the gender but also the politics of the candidates?

'50/50' proposals whereby every constituency would have one male and one female MP were orginally discussed in the context of a future Scottish assembly but are now gaining favour for Westminster with Tony Benn and Teresa Gorman. Such a system shares with Additional Member System the creation of two types of MP. And there are further problems. Most women candidates would surely prefer to know that they had been elected on merit in an open competition, not just as the best woman. Would the two MPs be likely to work as a team – sharing the constituency work on the basis of equality and expertise? Or would the female MP be regarded (by the other MP or by her party) as second class, albeit useful when tricky issues arise that the male MP would rather avoid? Unless the number of MPs at Westminster is to increase, then almost half the sitting male MPs would have to be disposed of to allow 325 women's seats to be established.

And what if voters would like to be represented by two women? Is it right to rule out, now, the possibility of ever having women fill more than half of the House of Commons?

WOMEN AND STV

The problem is not just how seats are filled, but the very existence of the single-member constituency seat. Any electoral system, proportional or otherwise, that relies on parties having to select (and voters having to vote for) a single candidate from each party will never enable a sizeable increase in women MPs. Only when a party has to draw up a balanced ticket of people to compete for, say three or four seats, will women be readily selected – and of course enabling the sitting MPs to stand again.

Even under First-Past-the-Post multi-member seats can allow more women into Parliament. Prior to 1950 there were such seats in Britain, and a number of women were elected who might otherwise not have reached Westminster. Barbara Castle became an MP in 1945 in the two-member seat of Blackburn: at the time, only 3.5 per cent of single seats were held by women, whereas nearly eight per cent of double or treble seats were.

The Single Transferable Vote system has the advantage of requiring multi-member constituencies which could encourage each party to put up a ticket which includes both male and female candidates. Voters can choose, in order of preference, candidates from the left or right wings of their own and other parties, or on the basis of a particular local or national issue. Most voters contribute positively to the election of at least one of their MPs, and the overall result is proportional, not just in terms of the distribution of seats to each party, but according to the voters' wishes. So women are empowered as voters.

The table shows that in Ireland the Dail has nearly 8 per cent women

(1989), which compares well with Britain, especially as there is still a problem getting women accepted as candidates in rural areas of the Republic and in the light of the dominant role of the Church. Ireland uses STV with multi-member constituencies electing between three and five MPs. Closer examination shows that the percentage elected in three member seats was only just over 5 per cent, but reached nearly 9 per cent in ones returning four or five members. In Australia under 7 per cent of the members of the lower house, which is elected by the Alternative Vote, are women; but of those elected to the Senate, using STV with an average of 5.4 member seats, over 22 per cent are women.

This may be because while voters allocate their preferences primarily on party lines, later preferences may go to other candidates using criteria like gender.[5] If four or five candidates are to be elected, voters' later preferences can have a significant effect: when only two or three are to be elected, voters' later choices are less likely to be taken up.

Furthermore, STV avoids the gender pitfalls of list systems and of the hybrid AMS. It recognises that being a woman (or man) is only one part of a person's identity and individuality and is not, therefore, the only criterion on which a person can be judged or elected. Whether or not women MPs are chosen will be up to the voters, not just the parties. Women must be enabled to play their full part in decision-making on all issues, and should be elected because of their political views on economics, defence, industry and so on – not just to bring a 'women's touch' to the debate.

Equally an electoral system cannot be judged simply by whether it can be used to increase women's representation. As Harriet Harman recently explained, it is not just about the right of women to be in Parliament – what matters is whether our system of government is working. Simply getting women elected is not the end of the story.

QUOTAS AND 'WOMEN'S ISSUES'

Parties, and other organisations, have begun positive action to encourage women. The parties will naturally go about this in different ways. The Conservative Party has used 'high flyer' conferences to educate and prepare women for taking part in electoral activity, but has generally shied away from any attempts to 'discriminate' in favour of women.

The introduction of quotas by Labour recognises that women are not starting out with the same advantages as their male colleagues. In 1990 the Party agreed an aim of 40 per cent women on its national bodies within 10 years. Quotas have also been introduced for elections to the shadow cabinet. Lesley Abdela, a past opponent of such measures, now reluctantly accepts the need for quotas, saying: 'The Berlin Wall of arcane recruitment methods, stereotyped criteria, blinkered vision and hundreds of years of male tradition will only be brought down with a sledgehammer such as the Jo Richardson rule.'

However, quotas carry the risk of sidelining women – into women's seats, women's sections, women's ministries and women's issues. It is ironic that Labour's 1991 conference which voted for quotas also threw Jo Richardson (who had pushed for this policy as well as for a Women's Ministry) and Barbara Switzer off the party's National Executive, leaving its constituency and trade union sections entirely without female representation.

The public sector union NUPE, the first trade union to introduce women's seats on its executive in the 1970s, has had rather more success. NUPE felt that simply getting a number of women onto the executive was not furthering the interests of the female membership of the union – mainly low-paid and part-time workers. In 1986 a new rule was introduced so that women can occupy a reserved seat for only two terms. Since then about 60 per cent of those elected to the women's seats have gone on to fight for the 'open' seats, and about 85 per cent of them have been successful.

So the system gives women a helping hand onto the executive, allowing them to gain the experience and reputation they need to fight future elections, but it recognises that having women in power does not automatically translate into policies which benefit women as a whole. This is true for government too.

Many observers felt that, as the first woman Prime Minister, Margaret Thatcher did very little for others of her sex. But it should be noted that women MPs have been behind important legislation which has benefited women. The Sex Discrimation Bill was first put forward by Joyce Butler in 1968, eventually taken over by Willie Hamilton and passed in 1972. In 1975 it was Barbara Castle who proposed the Equal Pay Bill.

'ADDING A FEW FEMALE INGREDIENTS ...'

There is a widespread hope that any opportunity to increase the number of women in politics will make a substantial difference to the style and quality of political life. Sue Innes in *Scotland on Sunday* has expressed the desire for a different politics to emerge with the introduction of a Scottish Parliament: 'Adding a few female ingredients to much the same cake is not what is wanted, nor just a bigger slice of it.' Such things are hard to judge, but it is likely that having a higher number of women in Parliament will make a difference to *the way* that issues are debated and even to *which* issues are debated.

Ray Michie, Liberal MP for Argyll & Bute, describes a debate on women's health in which she spoke along with women from all parties:

> I was extremely impressed with the knowledge in their speeches and I was also impressed with the sincerity on both sides of the House...It's a great sadness that there aren't more women in Parliament, because I do feel they have a greater response, a greater understanding of the issues which I think would be debated in a far better tempered manner.[6]

Parliament could come to have a new relevance to the lives of over half of the electorate. The possibility is increasingly of interest to the parties.

In a Fabian pamphlet Patricia Hewitt, former press secretary to Neil Kinnock, and Deborah Mattinson, a member of the advertising agency recruited to the Party's cause, suggest ways for Labour to attract women voters.[7] They identify the areas of policy women feel most strongly about – those on the 'social agenda' and those relevant to their experience of combining work and home responsibilities. They suggest this goes some way to explaining why in 1983 18 per cent of women switched their vote to the Conservatives following the sale of council houses, and why in 1987 11 per cent of young women switched back to Labour, as the Party's image as the most 'male' party began to change.

At the 1987 election, for the first time more women than men voted. To persuade these women to vote for a particular party, Hewitt and Mattinson argue, is not just a question of having policies that are important to women, but of 'speaking women's language', which among other things means making women MPs more visible. (Incidentally, they point out that the policies which would attract women are also popular among men!)

Although the political parties might encourage women into Parliament in order to win more of the sixteen million female votes, in the process they will probably be forced to carry through their election promises to women. Certainly the surprisingly loud outcry because John Major did not in 1991 pick any women for his Cabinet reflected a growing impatience with the lack of positive action by the parties to promote women. The 1990 MORI survey for the Electoral Reform Society showed that one of the reasons that women want PR is they think it would lead to the election of more women. In one year, the number of women saying they had heard of, or knew something about, PR had risen by 14 per cent; and of these, two-thirds wanted PR introduced for House of Commons elections. When asked why a system of PR would be preferable, they suggested it would be more worthwhile voting as fewer votes would be wasted. They thought they would have more control over the politicians, and expected more choice of candidates. They felt PR was more democratic, because seats would be won in proportion to votes, but also because they believed no government should have the support of less than half the electorate.

Winn Newman, a US 'equal pay for work of equal value' lawyer, studied 140 people who had changed sex. Those who had become men had increased their salaries. Those who had become women had seen their pay decrease. He therefore suggested there are two ways for women to achieve equality: either by taking the profit out of occupational segregation or by changing sex.

With political representation too, it is the system that creates profit for some by discriminating against women. And it is the political system which needs changing. The experience of having Mrs Thatcher as the 'best man in the cabinet' should have been warning enough against Mr Newman's other option – women with parliamentary ambitions opting for a sex-change!

NOTES

1 Quoted in Lesley Abdela, *Women with X Appeal*, Macdonald/Optima, London 1989.
2 Martin Pugh, *The Evolution of the British Electoral System*, Historical Association, London 1988.
3 Quoted in Fergus Finlay *Mary Robinson: A President With a Purpose*, The O'Brien Press, Dublin 1990.
4 See Beatrix Campbell, *The Iron Ladies: Why do Women Vote Tory?*, Virago, London 1987.
5 The transfer of second preferences, under an Alternative Vote system, was

crucial to the election of Mary Robinson as President of the Irish Republic in 1990. In her victory speech she played tribute to 'the women of Ireland who instead of rocking the cradle rocked the system'.

6 Lesley Abdela, *op.cit.*

7 Patricia Hewitt and Deborah Mattinson, *Women's Votes: The Key to Winning*, Fabian Society, London 1989.

11

A CURIOUS AMNESIA: THE FORGOTTEN LINK BETWEEN RULERS AND RULED

SARAH BENTON

On the harbour shore at Brixham, Devonshire, there is a small, drab statue. It stands on a square plinth, so ordinary and unimpressive that no one minds when passers-by sit on it to eat their chips, or dogs piddle on its corners. There is one odd thing about it: a plaque on the side informs you that the Queen unveiled that plaque, at that spot in June 1988.

Most people, if they read it at all, will look again in puzzlement. Why should the Queen herself travel all the way to Brixham to unveil a plaque on an old statue? They will look again and see that the statue is of Prince William of Orange, later King William III.

William of Orange, later of England, Scotland, Wales and, most bloodily, Ireland, arrived in his future realm on 5 November 1688. He touched down near Brixham with 500 ships and 14,000 troops, ready for what his advisers (who, Afghanistan-style, had 'invited' him in) feared might be a major battle for the throne. It was not. At some point, the statue records, he proclaimed: 'The Liberties of England and the Protestant Religion I Will Maintain.' History does not record what his wife Mary, the true heir, had to say. Some version of this tale is part of what is called Britain's Glorious Revolution.

Clearly, it never caught on. We celebrate 5 November not for the arrival of our liberator but for the death in 1606 of the Catholic Guy Fawkes. English tradition favours the tale of punishing Popish plots over that of a charter of political rights; the nondescript William III of English history has been claimed only by the Orangemen of Ireland

and Scotland as King Billy, hammer of the Catholics.

Remember Remember the Fifth of November

This was not always so. For one hundred years, the Glorious Revolution was celebrated in England. Every year, for instance, the Revolution Society met on 5 November to celebrate, in the words of the address in 1789, 'that event in this country to which the name of THE REVOLUTION has been given; and for which, for more than a century, it has been usual for the friends of freedom, and more especially Protestant dissenters, to celebrate with expressions of joy and exultation.'[1] By the 1780s, the tradition had been renewed by fresh pressure for political liberties and, in particular, for proper representation in Parliament, much of it initiated by a spate of new Revolution Clubs.[2] But what might have been – a continuous popular tradition from the seventeenth century, celebrating popular liberties, renewed in the 1780s – was broken. It was severed by the massive repression that followed news of the French Revolution, withering the development of the Enlightenment, dissenting and free-thinking. The socialist movement a further century on fashioned an alternative, syndicalist history, of protest against factory conditions, and of struggle for the eight-hour day, and to establish trade unions; it did not reconnect us to those old battles for political liberties. Robust republicanism had its last surge in Georgian England.

As a result of this break in history, there is a curious amnesia in England – England, not the UK – about its political history. England has a history as rich in popular political protest and demand as any of the European nations which, in 1989, took to the streets in joyous rediscovery of their own democratic traditions. In its political amnesia, England feeds instead on an ersatz diet of Country House history served up by the marriage of commerce and quangos. Even school history tends to begin a century after the Bill of Rights; modern Britain was 'made', not by its political passions, but by the sturdy industrial revolution.

As for its political libertarians, if it remembers Mary Wollstonecraft, it is because feminists have rescued her, needing to reclaim a women's history of desire for political rights. There has been no dynamic movement to reclaim Thomas Paine, who inspired her, and William Godwin, who married her. Both men, political ideologues of immense

importance in the history of democratic rights, are virtual strangers to
Britain today. When Britain's three party leaders named their political
heroes in November 1991, not one mentioned Paine or Godwin or
Wollstonecraft or John Milton or John Locke. Only Liberal Democrat
leader, Paddy Ashdown, included British political rights campaigners,
with the names of Emmeline Pankhurst and John Stuart Mill.[3] Even as
recent and as terribly English a socialist as Edward Carpenter, author
of *Towards Democracy*, is remembered as a Sheffield odd-ball, rather
than a celebrant of radical freedom, and a creator of a peculiarly
English democratic tradition.[4] And would William Morris enjoy his
rare fame if he were not incarnated in wallpaper in thousands of once
fashionable living rooms?

THE SLOUGH OF POLITICAL DESPOND

What has this got to do with contemporary English political culture
and the need for reform? The inspiration for popular political change is
always the retelling of a story in which the people have been
dispossessed of freedom and rights once theirs – and within their grasp
again if only they reach out for them. Mrs Thatcher knew this, and
alone among contemporary British political leaders made intensive use
of myths of English history. The making of such myths is essential to
counter the depression which dogs Britain's political life.

The principal bar to political change in modern democracies is not
the repressive power of the state but the sullenness of the people. This
is a state in which people do not know how things could be better, do
not believe things will change for the better, and show signs of
withdrawing from political society. The silence of sullenness cannot be
mistaken for contentment because of these signs of withdrawal. They
include an increasing hostility to paying taxes or contributing money
to the common good, a rising crime rate, a falling rate of electoral
registration and returns, a poor rate of involvement in public life and
an expressed contempt for political life. On 5 November 1991, Battle
in East Sussex did not celebrate the arrival of King Billy, nor even the
death of Guy Fawkes, but burnt in effigy the figures of John Major and
of Neil Kinnock – down with all politicians![5]

You could say that there is nothing new about this – a contempt for
politics has been common in Britain, and may even signal a healthy
irreverence for government. It has been common, but when it has

occurred it is usually a symptom of something wrong in political life. No European nation has drifted into the sort of political anomie which blights much of American public life, but to be complacent about the state of politics is foolhardy even in the terms of good right-wing management of society. It was during the long era of Conservative rule that people increasingly expressed their frustration through crowd violence; it was the supposedly contented English southerners who were most likely to disrupt council meetings with anger, sometimes violence, and occasionally obscenity about the poll tax. Campaigners against the poll tax in 1989 thought one reason for this was that the system of political representation, producing uniformly Conservative parliamentary voices in the South, was particularly frustrating for the millions of dissenting voices.[6]

Remaking Political Society

Conventional political theory tells us that political society is based on the mythical notion of a social contract: in exchange for protection of life and property and, perhaps, rights, we will consent to obey rules and accept the authority of government. Without this 'contract' there would be no political society.

This is not as wholly mythical as it seems. In one way or another, most generations remake their social contract. Our own times are peculiar because the generations preceding ours – say, the generations born between 1880 and 1930 – made their contracts in times of war. War demands exceptional qualities of government and people. War insists on the primacy of the public interest, on the significance of such potent political values as loyalty versus treachery, sacrifice versus selfishness. It is not surprising that, out of these social contracts, western governments were able to construct their welfare states.

Each generation must make its own contract. As the implicit bonds of corporate state and welfare state have broken down, various Prime Ministers have attempted to renew the contract in quite explicit, if very narrow, form. Harold Wilson, Prime Minister between 1974 and 1976, offered the Social Contract; his successor between 1976 and 1979, Jim Callaghan, offered the Social Compact. Mrs Thatcher's counter-revolution explicitly tore up the contract and declared the dissolution of political society. The man she set up to break the contract of the welfare state – 'blue-eyed boy' John Moore MP – spent a whole summer pondering how to do this. He announced his findings in a speech in September 1987 in which, amongst other things, he declared welfare was the responsibility of 'individuals and their families' and denounced the 'political' role of the many welfare societies, like the Child Poverty Action Group. It was the stubborn clinging to the welfare state contract by British citizens which, instead, broke John Moore.

John Major has attempted to recreate a contract with his Citizen's Charter and network of lesser charters around it. The ousters of Mrs Thatcher were aware of the potential breakdown of the political order – a decade of riots, and latterly of mass refusals to pay the poll tax, of voters disappearing from the electoral register, of the scandal of miscarriage of justice, and of state 'reforms' blocked by stubborn hostility to any action by his Government. A new order had been offered by the EC with its Social Charter. If Britain subscribed to this it would implicitly accept a contract between British citizens and the EC, thus giving the EC a direct political authority of its own. Major's Citizen's Charters acknowledge the welfare state contract, reassert the supreme authority of the British government, and also echo the old British royal practice of granting charters. These were granted to boroughs, or companies as licences to operate, and had little to do with political liberties. The advantage of remaking a social contract unilaterally and from above is that the government get the benefit of a renewed political order, but on its terms, without having a people confident of their ability to make political rights for themselves.

This is the problem with the new rights, and a problem which so far Charter 88 and all the political reform movements have not solved. There is no connection between them and the actual experience of needing a voice in Britain. A national campaign for constitutional reform, for instance, does not speak for, or to, those who are driven into apoplexy or despair by buses that do not run on time, or estates sinking under an intolerable burden of litter and broken windows. Without that connection, the danger of the movement for political reform is that it is run by, and for, those who are excluded from the political elite by the tight two party system. It will create space for the leaders of other parties and thwarted policy-makers; but it does not put itself at the head of an actual popular political movement for a fuller, more live democracy.

To which you might well say – 'But that movement does not exist. Let us then do what we can to expose the clubbish, hypocritical, secretive and sclerotic functioning of British politics, so that we too can declare, with the people of Zambia, that the days of elective dictatorship, hypocrisy and lies have given way to an era of democracy. Surely even a small, élite movement for political change is better than nothing?' To which the answer must be yes. But this will happen only when the institutional change is harnessed to a more powerful drive for social progress.

The Nature of Contemporary Protest

Compared with the famous 1960s, the end of the century has not been a time of unifying, mass national protest, focused on London and central powers. Political discontent emerges in a myriad of small, more local protests, and in the proliferation of non-national parties. By non-national I mean parties whose remit is either larger than the UK (notably the Greens) or confined to one region or 'sub-nation' within it (all the Northern Ireland Parties, the SNP and Plaid Cymru as well as the Cornish and Wessex parties and a few others).

This drift away from national organisation is likely to increase in inverse correlation to the development of transnational organisation (e.g. the EC). There are several further repercussions, including the emergence of sub-national groupings as the repressive lid of the nation-state is lifted, or as the nation-state is demonstrably unable to represent the interests of a special community, such as British fisheries.

So where are there signs of popular action which could be harnessed to a movement for political reform, and what sort of reform would best carry that movement onwards?

Among the numerous and varied issues over which people have organised in the last decade have been: police harassment of black people; women 'reclaiming the night' and opposing pornography; nuclear arms, especially cruise missiles; the American bases in Britain; new road and other large construction projects; toxic and nuclear waste dumping; the loss of local amenities, like a community centre or local open space; Islamic rights and identity; the poll tax; animal welfare action; representation for football fans. There has also been notable crowd violence at football matches, organised violence directed against the homes – literally the residence – of Asian people; the desecration of Jewish cemeteries and symbols; and the apolitical aggression of young men known as ram-raiders, lager louts, joy-riders, or football hooligans.

Clearly, all forms of discontent cannot be lumped together as protest at our political system. But the real damage to democracy is created when popular desires or demands simply cannot be represented in the existing system. This was true of the movement against the poll tax, in which the parliamentary Labour Party decided to excommunicate those involved in the anti-poll tax movement. It was also true of the mess over the route of the Channel tunnel rail route, in which Conservative Party discipline turned Kent Tory MPs into anxious go-betweens rather than effective popular leaders. Party discipline long ago replaced local representation as the principle of government.

THE TWO-PARTY SYSTEM

On the surface, problems of representation have not changed. A two-party system has survived the disintegrative forces which affected every developed country in the 1970s, when the collapse of party systems was predicted from Japan through Europe to the USA. But increasingly that system is 'out-of-sync' with the political and economic pressures on nation-state politics. Labour may only survive as the dominant party for the left because of the force of party discipline centrally, and because the voting system diminishes all the other contenders round the country.

In 1983, just 50.8 per cent, or fractionally over half of the electorate, voted for one of the two main parties. The other half either voted for one of the other parties, ranging from the Alliance, through the Nationalist parties to the marginal parties and group-ettes, or didn't vote at all (27.3 per cent). In 1987, the two-party system had improved its performance slightly with 55 per cent of the electorate voting for the two main parties, one fifth of the electorate voting for another party or group, and the non-voters falling back to 25 per cent. (As electoral registration in parts of the cities is notoriously poor, non-voters are in fact likely to comprise over one in four of the adult population, a proportion which intelligent estimates set higher following popular antipathy to liability for the poll tax.) Given that, structurally, everything is on the side of a high turn-out for one of two main parties, these figures hardly constitute a vote of confidence in the electoral system.

The peak of success for the two-party system was the 1950s, a period when it was happily seen as the apogee of responsible, democratic government. In the 1950 election for instance, the two parties got 77.5 per cent of the votes of the total electorate, and 89.5 per cent of those who actually voted. By 1966, 68 per cent of the electorate still voted for the two main parties, but the system was clearly past its peak. The figure in the February 1974 election was 59 per cent.

These figures are at least better than the American voting figures, where election turn-outs in the south have fallen to their lowest since the 1790s, and, despite a few 'third party' candidates at presidential elections, a dominant two-party system and a declining vote, seem to go hand in hand. As in Britain and Japan, the most striking loss to political society has been in the social democratic parties – the Democrats in the USA. In the USA the bias towards an exclusive two-party system has been built into the very structure of elections. Electoral law has been decided by individual states, although repeated Supreme Court challenges have created a more or less national system. Many states have both laid down specific requirements for a party to stand at all in elections (having received a certain number of votes previously, for instance) and, most notoriously, have had elaborate requirements for registering to vote, as well as physical difficulties, such as remote court houses operating erratic hours where would-be voters must go. In many states, people register as supporters of a party – rather than as citizens with the right to vote. In other words, the desire of the two main parties to dominate state powers and the popular vote have shaped – many would say distorted – the system of registration and voting.[7]

The system has been defended by those who want to exclude people (i.e., black voters, foreigners etc.) and political forces (socialists, trade unions) which appear to threaten the American way. These processes of exclusion do not affect political parties equally. The precipitous decline in voting in the USA has been among Democrats, rather than Republicans, just as the drift out of organised politics has been stronger among working-class and socialist voters in western Europe. Again, the threat to democracy is not, in the first place, due to 'the system', but to the lack of anything worth fighting for in politics among the dispossessed.

Why do the parties not do more to combat it? In the USA, a reason commonly cited by critical Democrats is that it is much easier for party leaders to 'work a system' based on a relatively small pool of known Democratic voters than to embrace a volatile and unpredictable mass of new voters, whose demands might jeopardise the smooth working of the administration. These potential new voters are, in essence, the urban black population and the poor who do not vote.[8] In Britain, neither the professional leadership, with their direct access to the mass media, nor the cadre-militants who run local parties, have a particular interest in running continuous mass membership campaigns. The mass membership campaign, initiated by Tribune and launched by Neil Kinnock and Gordon Brown in January 1988, failed in its objectives. The problem was not in recruiting people – Gordon Brown said this was easy;[9] the problem is sustaining their membership. What, after all, were they in the party for? What was the point of joining? The only answer to this was provided by Militant, which has claimed success in recruiting and holding members, as members of a narrowly-focused cadre organisation.

There are many reasons for the decline in party identification for social democratic parties, especially in Britain and the USA. They include the ceding of various party functions to the state (access to jobs and housing, for instance), the ceding to the mass media of the role of political information and education, the professionalisation of the party leadership, the shrinking of a hierarchical and/or unified working class, and the proliferation of other political identities and goals. But our current electoral and political system artificially maintains a two-party system, leaving only one party to represent at national, governmental level all the radical and dissenting voices in Britain.

THE PRINCIPLES OF REPRESENTATION

There is something amiss then with the working of the most fundamental principle of democracy, the representation of the people. The political parties, local authorities and Parliament exist as a convenient system of administration, not as a living democracy.

When world leaders talk complacently of the triumph of democracy, this is often understood to mean the principle that individual citizens delegate their civic authority to a representative government. But the idea that representation should be based on individuals, who would be grouped together in roughly equal numbers, emerged as a principle only in the late eighteenth century. In 1788, a year before the French Revolution, the Revolution Club of Leicester resolved 'that this town is improperly represented in Parliament'.[10] The idea that Parliament should represent the citizens and their beliefs was revolutionary. The reformers were inspired by the American debate[11] and were spurred on by the scandal of the Rotten Boroughs – old boroughs of England in particular which had few, or in the case of Old Sarum, no residents at all. Before the challenge from the revolution and constitutional clubs, few questioned that government, if it represented anything at all, represented either the town itself, regardless of numbers or the property interest. That being the case, universal voting was hardly an issue. It was assumed that the only 'rights' government would interfere with were those of property, and therefore only property owners needed representation.

From the 1780s, on and off for the next 120 years, mass suffrage movements challenged the right of the property-owning elite to govern the lives of the working class and the poor. They also challenged the very notion of what government did; over what it could exercise command. Thus the subsuming of women and servants into the male head of household, who alone had the right of representation, was not just because only the male head was seen as having 'a will of his own'; it was also because the lives of women and servants were seen as part of the male head's private domain, his, not the government's, to command.

The revolutionary implications of, first, the working-class suffrage movement, then the women's suffrage movement (and in the USA the long and uneven battle for black voting rights) have thus been immense. For they have not just opposed the elitism of the governing representatives. By putting themselves forwards as individuals with equal citizen rights, women, workers, black people have challenged the very foundations of representation and the sphere of government.

This did not lead immediately to the dissolution of collective forms of representation into a mass of equal individuals. For emerging out of the nineteenth-century ideas and experience came the dominant form of class politics. This adopted the party form of democratic government, but radically transformed the party. From the mid nineteenth century in the USA, and rather later in Europe, the political party was no longer the faction which organised patronage and intrigues and alliances; it became the embodiment of the popular will. For fifty to a hundred years, the political party displaced national assemblies as the representative of popular desire. Radicals who wanted change tried to change the party, rather than Parliament. This tradition ended up bashing its head against a brick wall in the Labour Party in the 1980s.

NEW FORMS OF REPRESENTATION

For the last two decades, political parties have been increasingly unable to represent the popular will. In the conflict between the party's role as actual or potential government and its role as representative of the people, the former won. In that victory, we in Britain have witnessed the shambles of the poll tax, in which both Conservative government and Labour opposition turned their backs on local protest for fear of seeming not to be in control. It is this most recent stage in the story of popular representation which is making the need for reform acute. And it is this which connects the story of popular rights and liberties to the current question about our forms of representation.

The form of political will. The problem is how to connect the actual forms of collective experience and interest which people have with forms of government and representation. For there can be no doubt that current forms of national and local state do not fit actually existing communities.

International. There is an urgent need for democrats, reformers, democratic socialists – all the bearers of the democratic tradition – to take the initiative on international democratic forms. If we accept, as most people now do, that many decisions have passed beyond the competence of national parliaments, then we have to make the links, have the talks, come up with the schemes which turn the idea of international democratic forums into a reality. MPs already form transnational groupings in the European Parliament. The parties themselves should create transnational organisations so that lay members can meet and debate with each other.

Regions and sub-nations. The Liberal Democrats and Labour Party are already committed to assemblies for Scotland, Wales and the English regions (whatever these are decided to be). These may well generate new political associations in those regions where there is a strong national or regional identity – Scotland obviously, south west England or East Anglia probably, the 'Home Counties' most doubtfully. Such new forms of political government – on the understanding the assemblies will have some administrative powers – will therefore vary in effectiveness according to local cultures and political feeling.

Cities and counties. Cities are unique communities, being significantly more cosmopolitan (anti-national) and pluralistic than any other political unit. Counties are increasingly irrelevant as representative forums. At best, they are sub-regional groupings, administrative units which are convenient to central government precisely because they do not carry a strong representative force.

Local community. It is at this level that some crucial forms of decentralisation must take place. Many of the 'house-keeping' decisions for local communities – sweeping the streets, local traffic control, community policing, use of parks and local amenities – should be handed over to those communities. They may make the wrong decisions, but bad decisions are better than apathy, cynicism and political alienation.

Nationally, there has to be representation for the non-geographic communities. If these cannot be incorporated into the existing party system, by, for instance, getting more representatives of Islamic, or black, or Asian, or female or young people into the mainstream parties, then there has to be the space for such interests to organise separately if they want to. That can only be assured by some sort of proportional representation. The danger of this is that politics 'balkanises' into what may be temporary political communities, but these 'fragments' are then institutionalised by a PR political system.

CONCLUSION

At the beginning of this century, the view that politics should represent class had superseded the eighteenth-century idea that politics represented towns and property interests, or more briefly, Court versus country. Each conflict produced party systems to match. This century, it seemed as though the two-party system was a mere reflection of great economic forces which set working class and ruling class in irreconcilable conflict with each other. In other words, economic interest decided who belonged to which political community.

The end of century fragmentation has changed all that. As class politics and the two-party system both weaken, new political leaderships emerge which help create new political communities. In other words, the emergence of a Green Party, or Plaid Cymru or an Islamic Party is not a mere mirror of a distinct Welsh or Muslim economic 'base'; rather, the new organisations show how political ideologists can create new political communities around an idea or notion of belonging. Whether or not they develop from their sectional or local roots depends on the objective need for their existence, the quality of their leadership and on whether the political system encourages their growth or seeks to abort them.

The argument in favour of a changed voting system, and new units of government, (i.e. empowered local communities, new regional assemblies, more powerful city governments) is that a decentralised system will better express the political will of different communities and, more importantly, it will allow those communities to develop a political will. This is the best counter to political depression and the withering of political society.

NOTES

1 Quoted in William St Clair, *The Godwins and the Shelleys*, Faber and Faber, London 1989. Edmund Burke's 'Reflections on the Revolution in France' was written as a response to the address given by Dr Price at this meeting of the Revolution Society, leading to Tom Paine's rebuttal, *The Rights of Man*.

2 Revolution clubs were set up before the French Revolution to 'reclaim' the 1688 revolution. But more were set up in 1789 to give support to, and adopt the demands of, the French Revolution. It was this linkage which so alarmed the government.

3 Neil Kinnock, Labour leader, named Nye Bevan, Mahatma Gandhi, Martin Luther King and Annie Besant; John Major, Conservative Prime Minister, named Iain Macleod, Pitt the Younger, William Gladstone, Neville Chamberlain and Stanley Baldwin; Paddy Ashdown named William Gladstone, Mahatma Gandhi, Emmeline Pankhurst and John Stuart Mill.

4 Carpenter was, of course, an odd-ball with his desire to link political freedom to a freedom of the body and sexuality. An utterly holistic writer, he does indeed seem anachronistic today; but his work is still moving to read.

5 Battle, landing site of the Norman conquerors, is one of many conservative commuter towns in which 'quaint' contemporary ceremonies are overlaid on almost forgotten traditions of a dissenting culture.

6 Interview with Edinburgh anti-poll tax group, July 1990.

7 There has been a lively debate in the USA over what is seen by the left as a calamitous collapse in civic culture and voting. There are various interpretations, of which one of the most persuasive is put by Frances Fox Piven and Richard Cloward in *Why Americans Don't Vote*, Pantheon Books, New York, 1989, which pinpoints the registration system. There are also sociological explanations, and the party-strategic analysis from Kevin Phillips, who explains the shift to Republicanism as in part a result of conscious Republican strategy, though this does not explain the falling vote.

8 Robert Kuttner explores the problems of Democrat renewal in *The Life of the Party*, New York, 1988.

9 Interview with SB, September 1988.

10 John Stevenson, *Popular Disturbances in England, 1700–1870*, Longman, Harlow 1979.

11 For an interesting discussion on this, which unfortunately sees nothing in the absence of women voters, see the classic work by J.R. Pole, *Political Representation in England and the Origins of the American Republic*, Macmillan, London 1966.

12

SOMEBODY DOES IT BETTER: PR IN THE BUILDING OF THE EUROPEAN COMMUNITY

DAVID MARTIN

The European Community (EC) operates by way of political institutions based on proportionality through which consensus is sought. I believe this method of operation offers the best way forward for the citizens of the Community, and, perhaps, a model for the rest of the world.

The European Community aims at a federal system based on the principle of 'subsidiarity', meaning that decisions are taken at the lowest possible level. We are moving towards a European Union built on the sovereignty of the citizen, where any centralising tendency is counterbalanced by a Europe of the Regions. Power moves down as well as up and is always controlled by the people.

In economic policy, the Community seeks a balance between the free market and regulation. The free market ethos is designed to ensure that EC goods can compete in world markets and to create the wealth needed to sustain an adequate standard of living while improving social provision into the twenty-first century. Regulation is needed to guard against monopoly, ensure the fruits of the market are distributed fairly throughout the Community and that there are minimum standards in the workplace – to do this the EC needs comprehensive regional and social policies. It appeared from Maastricht that the British Government was prepared to let the market rip: once again our national government resisted consensus, and remained in a confrontational, isolated position, at variance with modern European thinking.

It is apparent to most political observers on the continent that the nation state is both too small and too large to deal with the geo-political changes taking place in the global and local economy: too small to deal with competition from the USA and Japan: too large to be flexible enough to deal with the disparities in peripheral economies. We therefore need institutions to cope with these opposite, yet complementary, movements. We need European Union to deal with the central issues, and we need a Europe of the Regions to balance any centralising tendencies. To achieve such a system we will need an increased pooling of nation-state sovereignty. This can only be achieved by maximum consensus and co-operation.

In operating a system designed to bring along as many people as possible, the progress of the Community has often seemed painstakingly slow, often halting, even going into reverse. However, the European Community has been one of the great success stories of the twentieth century, bringing together countries which previously formed the cockpit for two major conflagrations. Not only working together to create the wealth that will pay for the social programmes the citizens of the Community desire, but also making a contribution to the eradication of poverty throughout the world.

The European Community might yet provide a model for other areas of the world – Africa, Asia, Central and South America, the former Soviet Union – where national and ethnic differences are tending to drive people apart. At the very least the European Community could offer a third way between the failed Soviet regime and the rampant capitalism of both the USA and Japan.

As well as having what I hope will be a progressive influence on a world level, the operation of EC politics has the potential to influence the future operation of British politics in a positive way.

PROGRESS BY WAY OF PROPORTIONALITY

Within the European Community, eleven out of twelve member states use a system of proportional representation for domestic elections and for elections to the European Parliament at Strasbourg. Only one member state, the United Kingdom, uses a First-Past-the-Post voting system (except for Northern Ireland, where PR is used for local elections and European elections). Informed opinion within the UK is now increasingly in favour of PR for elections to the European

Parliament, and some form of PR is likely to be used for European elections in 1994 throughout the whole of the UK.

A form of proportionality has also been introduced into the proceedings of the Council of Ministers. The Single European Act, which came into force in July 1987, introduced qualified majority voting for measures connected with the creation of the Single European Market. This gives each member state a weighting according to the size of its population: France, Germany, Italy and the UK have ten votes each; Spain has eight; Belgium, Greece, the Netherlands and Portugal have five each; Denmark and Ireland have three and Luxembourg two. Out of a possible seventy-six votes, fifty-four constitutes a qualified majority. Such a system facilitates the building of coalitions and speeds up the legislative process. The European Parliament would like to see qualified majority voting for social and environmental measures; this would, for example, have made it impossible for Mrs Thatcher to block the Social Charter, or for Mr Major to opt out of the Social Chapter.

The building of coalitions is also necessary within the European Parliament. Although the Socialist Group is the largest in the Parliament, with 180 members out of the 518, there are another nine political groups and ten non-attached members. There is no overall majority within the chamber and thus a need to form alliances. At the same time, the committee structure of the European Parliament enhances the need for Euro-MPs to take a longer-term view of strategy than at Westminster. Influencing legislation involves negotiation as well as anticipating the reactions of coalition partners and opponents alike. A good example of this is the processing of the overall EC budget, in which the Strasbourg Parliament has real power.

This is particularly the case with farm spending, where specific groupings emerge to scrutinise and vote on the hundreds of amendments put to the Commission's original plan. Unusual alliances emerge between MEPs of normally hostile parties, coming together with others who represent farming communities to help their constituents on a range of subject areas from meat, cereals, dairy, and wine production to sugar beet, olive oil and tobacco. Equally united, against them, will be cross-party groupings negotiating to get funds diverted from agricultural spending to regional and social policies which assist employment in run-down traditional industrial areas, or to investment in new technology projects. This is the Strasbourg Parliament at its best, when it has real power, working for those who elected it, across political and national barriers.

European parliamentary politics therefore emphasise the building and maintenance of coalitions. There is a greater need for compromise and conciliation than at Westminster, where engagement is usually confrontational and exclusive.

The average Euro-MP tends to have more influence within the European Parliament than a backbench MP in the House of Commons. For the Euro-MP, there is a much greater chance of influencing policy provided he or she is willing to compromise with colleagues who may be in a different party. The Environmental Committee is a good example here. The introduction of lead-free petrol can be traced back to a resolution tabled by the Environment and Transport Committees in 1981. In April 1989, using increased powers given us under the Single European Act, Parliament voted by 309 votes to five to urge the Council of Ministers to grant new emission controls introducing more efficient engines and catalytic converters for most cars.

Labour Euro-MPs have a particularly good chance of influencing events through the size of our group and our participation in the coalition known as the Socialist Group – it was a Labour Euro-MP, Ken Collins, who chaired the Environment Committee. At Westminster, Labour MPs can only criticise from the Opposition benches, which seems a great waste of talent and effort.

In one sense the sheer volume of legislation emanating from the European Community is bound to alter the way British government operates. This legislation requires detailed scrutiny and cannot be dealt with effectively by adversarial-style politics. Members of the House of Commons will be required to come together much more in committee, to deal with this legislation, which in itself will lead to the building of coalitions and the breakdown of some party-political hostility.

A CULTURE OF CONSENSUS

When I was elected leader of the British Labour Group in the European Parliament in June 1987 I readily acknowledged that I had changed my mind on the EC. I resolved to use that year to argue vigorously for a change in Labour Party attitude to the EC even though I knew I would probably lose the leadership for my efforts. I reasoned that it was time to take a positive approach towards the EC: the world had moved on since 1975, and there was no way we were going to withdraw. It was imperative that we ceased the sterile 'in out' argument, and united around a policy of winning economic and social improvements for our people from the EC while at the same time arguing for democratic reform which would make such a process more fruitful. I put my ideas on this subject into a Fabian pamphlet entitled *Bringing Common Sense to the Common Market – A Left Agenda for Europe* (London, March 1988). Although, unfortunately, I was right in my prediction about losing the leadership, I believe the pamphlet had the desired effect. Indeed Richard Owen and Michael Dynes comment in the *Times Guide to 1992* that the abandonment of the previous commitment to withdrawal from the EC was the key change in Labour's policy review: the 'intellectual ground for that change was prepared in a Fabian pamphlet written by David Martin MEP, then leader of the Labour Group in Strasbourg.'[1]

In his foreword to my book *Europe: An Ever Closer Union*, Bernard Crick observes that it is perhaps easier for a Scot to think positively about European federalism because a Scot 'already knows that it is easily possible, indeed often enriching, to have graduated or relative allegiances, not all or nothing: Scottish *and* British, British *and* European'. Crick goes on to say: 'None of us will lose our national identities; they will simply be less attached to monopolistic and mutually hostile centralised states.'[2] This was a very astute perception and a very European way of thinking. Both my experience of the Scottish Constitutional Convention and of the European Parliament has led me to believe that consensual politics is preferable to, and, in many cases, much more fruitful than Britain's traditionally confrontational politics. In many ways Scottish experience and thinking is closer to the intellectual endeavour of mainstream continental Europe, a phenomenon that stretches back to the Scottish Enlightenment and beyond.

Before saying something about the Scottish way of thinking it is important to point out a connection that I think exists between the case put by the Scottish Constitutional Convention for the establishment of a Scottish Parliament within the UK and the EC, and the concepts of European Union and a Europe of the Regions; and so why people in Scotland are more positive about European Union than some people in England. This is not to be blind about the faults of the EC: I have previously pointed out the similarities between over-centralisation of UK government in the Prime Minister's Office and the secretive nature of the Council of Ministers.[3]

The specific problem at the heart of Scottish and European debate is not shrinking sovereignty, as portrayed by Mrs Thatcher in her Bruges speech, but the democratic deficit. The way forward for Scotland and the EC is to make all European competencies the legitimate preserve of the European Parliament, which would be directly accountable to the people who elect it; and similarly to make Scottish affairs the preserve of a Scottish Parliament and so accountable to the people of Scotland.

We Scots have already experienced a Union. The Union with England in 1707. This Act led to economic and social benefits for the Scottish people and preceded the cultural and intellectual flowering of the Scottish Enlightenment when thinkers like David Hume, Adam Smith, Adam Ferguson and Thomas Reid contributed so much to European thought. However, it is now almost universally accepted that we got the political settlement wrong. The Scottish people should have retained their Parliament within the British Union, as was argued by Andrew Fletcher (1655-1716), who sat in the Scots Parliament in 1681 and whose proposed 'limitations' aimed at constructing a federal instead of incorporating a union. Britain has need of an Andrew Fletcher today. I and many of my colleagues in the Scottish Constitutional Convention are excited by the prospect that the process of European Union and the development of a Europe of the Regions offers the possibility of redressing the political imbalance of the 1707 Union through a federal Britain in a federal Europe. The lesson we have learned could be useful too for European Union.

In Scotland our cross-cultural continental links predate the 1707 Union of parliaments with England and the flowering of the Scottish Enlightenment (1730-1780). Scottish medical schools and universities owe much to the continental European model as does our legal system. Scots law, education and religious institutions were entrenched by the Treaty of Union and the accompanying Act of Security, and survived the Union as independent entities.

The Scottish religious and education systems have an egalitarian, democratic philosophy running through them. The contemporary Scots philosopher and historian of ideas, George Davie, has made the case for the Scottish 'democratic intellect' in his book of that title.[4] Scottish education has been traditionally more broad-based and comprehensive than English education. Davie also points out that the Scottish 'common sense' school of philosophy championed by Thomas Reid (1710-1796) had much more in common with the continental school of thinkers such as the French philosopher Descartes, who

'Oh, no! Euro-sceptics!'

Nick Newman, *The Spectator*, 23 November 1991. © *The Spectator*, 1991. Reproduced by kind permission.

believed in the innateness of ideas, than with the *tabula rasa* school of philosophers such as those represented by John Locke.

Sir James Stewart, in his *Enquiry into the Principles of Political Economy* of 1767, was keen to point out the limitations and insularity of England, and thus make a comparison between the English and the Scottish connection to the Continent. He attacked the shortsightedness of English pragmatism. It might be said that, whereas someone like John Major is more at home with the English empirical analytical method of reasoning, John Smith, a Scots lawyer by training, though possessing an extremely analytical mind, is equally at home with the more speculative continental frame of mind.

Davie also points out that not only was Scottish thinking and society influenced by continental experience, but that it was a two-way flow. Scottish Enlightenment thinking had more influence on the Continent than it did in England: Kant was woken from his 'dogmatic slumbers' by Hume; Thomas Reid was an influence on the French phenomenologists.

It is these intellectual cross-cultural currents between Scotland and the Continent which give us the ability to work in the more consensual and far-seeing institutions established within the European Community.

The democratic and egalitarian nature of Scots society is also derived from our Calvanist religious history. The lay member make-up of the Scots presbytery and non-established nature of the Scottish Church makes it much more in touch with the people. Jean Jacques Rousseau based many of his arguments for direct democracy (which he argued could not exist in a state bigger than Corsica) on his perception of the functioning of the Calvanist system in Switzerland, which has a federal structure. Many Scots, brought up in a Calvinist tradition, were inspired by the ideas of Rousseau and the French Revolution.

Mrs Thatcher experienced what can only be described as 'culture shock' when she came to deliver her 'Sermon on the Mound' on 21 May 1988 to the General Assembly of the Church of Scotland, which meets on the Mound in Edinburgh. Scottish Church leaders were anxious to dissociate themselves from Mrs Thatcher's materialistic message. They were also unhappy with the British Government's opposition to the European Social Charter, which sought to guarantee minimum rights and standards to working people and which was very much in tune with Scottish thinking, especially among the Churches.

'WE, THE PEOPLE'

The Scottish Churches have been heavily involved in the Constitutional Convention. Canon Kenyon Wright, Chair of the Executive Committee, outlined the Convention's purpose in asserting the Declaration of the Claim of Right on 30 March 1989 (from the same building Mrs Thatcher had delivered her 'Sermon on the Mound'):

> We gathered as a Constitutional Convention do hereby acknowledge the sovereign right of the Scottish people to determine the form of government best suited to their needs and do hereby declare and pledge that in all our actions and deliberations their interests shall be paramount.

Kenyon went on to raise the rhetorical question: 'What if that other voice that we all know so well says "We are the state and we say no"?' His answer was unequivocal, and very Scottish: 'We are the people and we say yes.'

Any Scottish Parliament which emerges from the work of the Scottish Constitutional Convention will be based on the modern European model, not the antiquarian Westminster model. And no bad thing. The electoral system for the Parliament will not be First-Past-the-Post. It will, I believe, be proportional. Proportional representation prepares the ground for consensual politics. By its very nature progress based on consensual politics is more permanent, and at less risk of being overturned by a subsequent administration.

My experience of the European Community leads me to believe that it provides a good model for electoral reform in the UK. This is not to say there is no need for reform of the EC to make it much more democratic, but I have argued that case elsewhere:[5] here I want to emphasise the positive elements of the European scene in order to see how we could benefit from emulating it. Stated baldly, the ethos of EC institutions is collective, its method consensual and its representation proportional; the ethos of the UK parliamentary system is individualist, its method confrontational and its representation based on 'winner takes all'.

Adversarial politics, in my experience, reinforce entrenched positions. If you want to dig yourself out of that trench you need to build consensus. Confrontation is not the best way to convert others to your point of view. Antagonistic debate can have the benefit of displaying both sides of an argument so that a reasoned decision can be taken, but opposition for opposition's sake can be extremely futile. During my first term in the European Parliament some of my comrades tried to convince our continental colleagues of the lunacy of Community politics by way of megaphone diplomacy. Their siren voices succeeded only in drawing themselves onto the rocks.

Mrs Thatcher's views on Europe and proportional representation were very similar to those of these comrades. Mrs Thatcher personified confrontation. The abrasive iron lady failed in Europe, was rejected in Scotland and ultimately scrapped by her own Party. Her attitude to the Social Charter, carried on by John Major, drew the clearest distinction between the British and the European attitudes to politics. It precipitated a change in attitude towards the EC, and a willingness to co-operate with their continental colleagues, among many Labour and trade union representatives in Britain.

A True Community

The Social Charter, which became the Social Action Programme and is now referred to as the social chapter, can best be understood in its original formulation as the 'social dimension'. The idea behind the social dimension was that the free market deregulatory measures introduced to produce the Single Market in 1992 are not enough to achieve a true European Community, and, in some respects, would make such an aim more difficult by increasing the divisions between rich and poor, between capital and labour. The Social Charter was therefore an attempt to codify what was necessary, in terms of legislation, to turn the European *Economic* Community into a European Community where all citizens would benefit from the Single Market.

The Social Charter lies at the heart of the change in attitude towards the European way of doing things. It divides Thatcherites off from the rest and helps redefine socialism in a European context. If the European Parliament had been the democratic core in the EC, the Social Charter would have been in place now: there was a massive majority in favour at Strasbourg. Jacques Delors' speech on the Social Charter to the British Trades Union Congress (TUC) Conference at Bournemouth in September 1988 was a watershed, marking a new respectability which the Charter had given EC politics on the left in Britain. Delors told the assembled trade unionists: 'It is impossible to build Europe only on deregulation ... The internal market should be designed to benefit each and every citizen of the Community.' The same month, when speaking to West German trade unionists and business executives in Cologne, Delors called for a 'new Keynes or Beveridge' to lay down a comprehensive EC social and employment programme for 1992, together with a plan for wealth redistribution.

But even before that overt call for an EC social policy the contrast between Mrs Thatcher's attitude and that of politicians such as President Mitterrand and Chancellor Kohl was revealing. On 27 June 1988 – the day Jacques Delors was reappointed as President of the European Commission – Francois Mitterrand attacked Mrs Thatcher's reluctance to back moves to protect workers' rights: 'Europe cannot separate itself from its workers. I cannot be part of a Europe which does nothing in the social sphere.' To which Mrs Thatcher responded: 'Talk of dialogue with the social partners is old fashioned': it was better to talk to the workers 'like colleagues in one's own firm. The key thing is to increase their prosperity and make them owners of capital and property.'

Whereas Mitterrand argued that he did not want a Europe that gave nothing to the workers, Mrs Thatcher presumably considered us 'Brits' as employees in UK plc, and she, as managing director, would look after our interests thank you very much. Nothing was said about our 'ex-colleagues' – the unemployed.

The ideological rifts with the French Socialist Mitterrand were to be expected but what must have come as a shock to Thatcher was to find that the rightwing German Chancellor, Helmut Kohl, was one of the Social Charter's stoutest advocates. As Lutz Stavenhagen, the German cabinet minister responsible for European affairs, put it at the time:

> Chancellor Kohl feels that to run a country, or to run a company, makes it necessary to operate on consensus. You can't operate on conflict. After 1992 we don't want just to have an open market-place. The Single European Act must include a social side. There have to be minimum rules and minimum rights.

While the British Government was advertising the creation of the European Single Market as '1992 Open for Business', Chancellor Kohl was convening a Social Partner Conference with employers, trade unions and consumer groups to build a German consensus around 1992.

Despite Mrs Thatcher's rantings, many Conservative voters in the UK could see nothing 'Marxist' about what Mrs Thatcher called the 'Socialist Charter'. Some Conservative politicians realised that the bulk of it had been part of the accepted consensus in the UK since the end of the Second World War. Both Michael Heseltine and Lord Plumb, the British Conservative President of the European Parliament, condemned what they saw as the British Government's unconstructive attitude. Edward Heath was, as usual, one of the most outspoken of the Government's critics.

But bewilderment came not just from the left of the Conservative Party – Alasdair Hutton, then Euro-MP for the South of Scotland, believed 'nine tenths of the Charter wholly unexceptional'. In good businesses in Scotland, he argued, close consultations already took place between management and workers, and only in the 'odd Victorian companies' were there significant problems. Alasdair Hutton felt that as far as the Charter's social security and anti-discriminatory proposals were concerned, 'there can be no real objections to most of them'. He clearly thought the Conservative Government's opposition to the Social Charter was a vote-loser. He was right: along with many of his colleagues, he went on to lose his seat at the June 1989 Euro-elections.

In the Council of Ministers right, left and centre governments voted eleven to one in favour of the Social Charter. In the European Parliament rightwing Christian Democrats voted with the Socialist Group and Communist Euro-MPs to support the Charter. Only the UK Conservatives and European fascists opposed in any great numbers.

The battle over the Social Charter demonstrated the possibility of breaking the hegemony of the right in Britain. Electoral reform could make the loss of the Conservative's exclusive hold on the levers of government permanent. There is substantial cross-party support for social progress in the UK as there is throughout the EC. Mrs Thatcher could never have enforced her convictions on an unconvinced majority of the UK electorate if we had had proportional representation in Britain; she would not have been able to roll back the frontiers of the welfare state in Britain, nor hold up up social progress for the rest of the EC.

REPRESENTATION AND DIVERSITY

The way to achieve electoral reform for the UK is to push for it at EC elections, for which the Community treaties specify there should be a uniform electoral procedure. Unlike other areas of Community law, where the Commission has the right to make proposals to the Council of Ministers, the Treaty of Rome provides in this case for the European Parliament to draw up a proposal which can only be adopted if supported unanimously in the Council. Parliament produced such a proposal in 1983 (the Seitlinger Report) but Council was unable to reach agreement.

It is not just legal requirements which motivate the Parliament. Many members feel that having twelve different electoral systems for a single Parliament creates unacceptable distortions. In particular, the results in one member state whose electoral system is not proportional determine the overall political balance in the Parliament to a greater extent than the results in any other. In the UK a five per cent swing from left to right or vice versa will produce a disproportional shift of perhaps twenty of the total eighty-one seats. Labour has swung from having only seventeen Euro-MPs in 1979 to having forty-five in 1989, with only a relatively small change in the percentage vote received. In both cases Labour was the second largest socialist party, but in one case ended up being only a minor part of the Socialist Group and in the other becoming its most important component. It is essentially unfair that the overall balance in the European Parliament depends more on the election results in one state than in any other.

The most recent attempt to move towards a unified system of proportional representation for the European Parliament took place in the October 1991 when the Parliament debated a report from the institutional affairs spokesman on the issue, Belgian Liberal Euro-MP Karel De Gucht. De Gucht's approach is to try to establish common principles rather than lay down a detailed system – the rock on which earlier attempts to float a unified system had floundered.

The Parliament voted 150 to twenty-six, with thirty-eight abstentions, in favour of a new electoral system organised on the basis of proportional representation. Only myself and the Conservative Euro-MP for Sussex West, Madron Seligman, among the British members, voted in favour. Twenty-nine British Euro-MPs abstained. Voting against were four Conservatives – Christopher Beazley (Cornwall & Plymouth), Margaret Daly (Somerset & Dorset West),

Paul Howell (Norfolk), and Edward Kellett-Bowman (Hampshire Central); and five Labour members – Alex Falconer (Mid Scotland & Fife), Eddie Newman (Greater Manchester Central), Alex Smith (South of Scotland), Llewellyn Smith (South East Wales) and Ken Stewart (Merseyside West). Among the abstainers, Derek Prag (Conservative, Hertfordshire) said he was not against proportional representation as long as there was some means of keeping the constituency system and maintaining close links with voters. My colleague Geoff Hoon (Derbyshire) referred to Labour's review of electoral systems and argued that efforts should first be made to change the attitude of national parties. All in all, and despite the sceptics, I felt the debate marked progress.

Electoral reform in the UK allowing for proportional representation in European elections will make the Strasbourg Parliament more representative and efficient; and hence an even greater contrast to Westminster. I hope for a similarly representative parliament in Scotland. Both will strengthen the case for a UK Parliament which reflects the full diversity of British public opinion.

NOTES

1 Richard Owen & Michael Dynes, *The Times Guide to 1992: Britain in a Europe Without Frontiers – a comprehensive handbook*, Times Books Ltd, London 2nd edition 1990.
2 David Martin *Europe an Ever Closer Union*, Spokesman, Nottingham 1991.
3 'The Democratic Deficit', in Owen Dudley Edwards (ed.), *A Claim of Right for Scotland*, Polygon, Edinburgh 1989.
4 George Elder David, *The Democratic Intellect – Scotland and her Universities in the Nineteenth Century*, Edinburgh University Press, Edinburgh 1961.
5 David Martin, *European Union and the Democratic Deficit*, John Wheatley Centre, Broxburn 1990.

13

LOCAL GOVERNMENT: THE DECLINE OF THE ONE-PARTY STATE

STEVE LEACH AND CHRIS GAME

First-Past-the-Post and the resulting two-party parliamentary dominance have left Westminster politicians with little experience of anything other than single-party governments. To them, the negotiation and operation of inter-party pacts and coalitions are foreign activities – in all senses of the phrase.

Yet at local level, even under the same electoral system, hung councils and power-sharing administrations are commonplace. In many areas they are permanent features of political life. Can we therefore, by analysing the behaviour of these hung authorities, gain some insights into what might happen in a hung (or balanced[1]) Parliament which would become more usual under a proportional voting system?

It is a seductive idea, especially for those of us with a professional interest in fostering the study of local government and politics. But it has a limited mileage. Just as local government elections are less useful indicators of national voting intentions than well-conducted national opinion polls, so hung councils are far from ideal predictive models for hung Parliaments.

When it comes to specifics, the institutional and constitutional differences between the two levels of government are mostly too great for meaningful parallels to be drawn. For pointers to parliamentary practice, it may be at least as instructive to look at the extensive experience elsewhere in Europe of national coalition and minority government – as, for example, does David Butler in his fascinating book *Governing Without a Majority*.[2]

But it is enlightening *in general terms* to see the many, often inventive, ways in which previously dyed-in-the-wool local party adversaries manage to work together when a council's voting mathematics demand it. There may even be a message here for some of our parliamentary leaders.

THE RISE OF THE HUNG COUNCIL

Ever since the 1974 reorganisation of local government outside London, between one in three and one in four councils have generally been hung (see Table 13.1). We define a hung authority as one in which a majority of councillors are attached to political parties, but in which no party holds a majority of seats.

Table 13.1   Hung Councils as a Proportion of All 'Partisan' Councils*

	1974 (%)	1986 (%)	1990 (%)	1991 (%)
England and Wales				
London Boroughs (32)	3	12	9	9†
Metropolitan Districts (36)	14	22	8	8
County Councils (47)	37	53	26	26†
District Councils (333)	34	29	30	35
Total	29	30	26	29
Scotland				
Regions & Islands (12)	17	33	50	50†
District Councils (53)	10	17	28	28†
Total	27	22	31	31†

Notes:
* 'Partisan' refers to a situation in which over 50 per cent of the seats on a council are held by members of political parties or groups. 'Hung' refers to a situation in which no single party group on a 'partisan' council holds over 50 per cent of the seats.
† Councils for which no elections were held in May 1991.

Perhaps the two most striking increases in these numbers came in 1985 and 1991. The 1985 county council elections left twenty-five of the forty-seven English and Welsh county councils without clear majorities. Since May 1991 significantly more shire districts have been hung (105) than are under either Conservative (79) or Labour (95) majority control.

Those 1991 elections were noted for the exceptional, and largely unexpected, performance of the Liberal Democrats, who made net gains of over 500 seats and took overall control of some seventeen new councils. But just as remarkable were the number of former Conservative strongholds which became hung, often for the first time in their history: Solihull MBC, Bournemouth BC, Brentwood DC, Canterbury City, East Hampshire DC, Guildford BC, New Forest DC, Reigate & Banstead BC, Stratford-on-Avon DC, Waverley BC, Winchester City, and Windsor & Maidenhead DC.

Novel though the hung experience may have been for some of these councils, it is clearly a familiar enough phenomenon in British local government. What has changed since 1974 is the nature and character of hung authorities, rather than their overall numbers. Until the late 1970s, many – probably most – hung councils were 'low partisan' in nature, with a significant proportion of Independents and a style of operation which played down the role of party politics. Being arithmetically hung presented no great problems.

It was only really in the 1980s, as local government became steadily and more overtly party-politicised, that the hung council came to be seen as a management challenge for officers and members alike. Reports began to appear in the local government press of some of the positive and negative features – genuinely vote-swaying council debates, marathon budget-setting meetings – of life on hung councils such as Bradford, Bedfordshire, Berkshire, Cheshire, Leicestershire, and Lothian Region.

By 1987, as we described in *Co-operation and Conflict*,[3] almost two-thirds of the 128 technically hung councils in Great Britain were highly politicised: the great majority of their councillors were publicly acknowledged members of political parties. The proportion will have risen at least slightly since then.

The principal force fuelling interest in these councils has been the local electoral impact of, successively, the Liberal Party, the SDP, the Alliance, the Democrats, and now the Liberal Democrats, who have consistently performed better in local elections than their national opinion poll ratings would imply. It is not surprising that they have most welcomed hung authorities, seeing them as opportunities for sharing power in ways they can only dream of nationally. In 138 councils (at time of writing) the Liberal Democrats have either majority party control or minority party influence – with the latter outnumbering the former by about five to one.

THE HUNG COUNTIES 1985-89: SIX KEY CHANGES

The Alliance parties made most of the early running in politicised hung councils and were most concerned to try to 'make them work'. More recently, there have been signs of the other major parties developing their own approaches which are more accepting of, and more appropriate to, the hung situation. From detailed analysis of the twenty-five hung county councils during the period from 1985-89, we have identified six key changes in the *modi operandi* of the parties. These six developments are by no means universally evident, but do represent definite trends.

From 'Minority Administration' to 'No Administration'
Table 13.2 shows the major changes in forms of administration across the twenty-five counties during the four-year period after May 1985. In no fewer than ten of these councils, there were changes either in the party holding the committee chairs – e.g. from a minority Conservative to a minority Labour administration – or in the actual form of administration. Depending on one's point of view, this may be seen either as a depressing confirmation of their inherent instability, or as an encouraging demonstration of the parties' capacity to learn from their early mistakes.

In the immediate aftermath of the 1985 elections, each of the three parties made their own characteristic mistakes. When first encountered with a hung situation, both Labour and Conservative parties tended to act as if the situation didn't exist. They would push for the formation of a single-party administration, as if this would recreate the familiar certainties of majority control.

Labour's characteristic mistake, particularly in situations in which it was the largest party, was to pursue a 'governmental strategy': arguing they would take the chairs of committees *only* if they were guaranteed a majority on all committees. Grounded in experience of majority control, this strategy reflected the view that any effective governmental role was otherwise impossible. In Cumbria and Humberside the strategy

145

Table 13.2 Major Changes in the Forms of Hung County Administrations, 1985-89

	May 1985		April 1989
AVON	Minority Labour	→	No Administration – *ad hoc* chairs
BEDFORDSHIRE	No Administration		No Administration – *ad hoc* chairs
CAMBRIDGESHIRE	Minority Alliance	→	No Administration – technical chairs
CHESHIRE	Minority Labour		Minority Labour
CORNWALL	Shared Power		Shared Power
CUMBRIA	Minority Labour		Minority Labour
DEVON	Minority Alliance	→ →	No Administration – *ad hoc* chairs
EAST SUSSEX	Conservative – 'knife-edge'		Conservative – 'knife-edge'
ESSEX	Minority Conservative		Minority Conservative
GLOUCESTERSHIRE	Minority Alliance		Minority Democrat
HAMPSHIRE	Conservative – 'knife-edge'		Conservative – 'knife-edge'
HERTFORDSHIRE	Minority Conservative	→ →	Minority Labour
HUMBERSIDE	Minority Conservative		Minority Labour
LANCASHIRE	Minority Labour		Minority Labour
LEICESTERSHIRE	Minority Conservative	→	No Administration – *ad hoc* chairs
NORTHAMPTONSHIRE	Conservative – 'knife-edge'		Conservative – 'knife-edge'
NORTHUMBERLAND	Minority Labour	→	Shared Power (excl. Labour)
NORTH YORKSHIRE	Conservative – 'knife-edge'		Conservative – 'knife-edge'
OXFORDSHIRE	Minority Conservative	→ →	No Administration – rotating chairs
SHROPSHIRE	Minority Labour		Shared Power
SOMERSET	Minority Alliance		Minority Democrat
WARWICKSHIRE	Minority Labour		Minority Labour
WILTSHIRE	Minority Alliance		Minority Democrat
CLWYD	Shared Power (excl. Labour)		Shared Power (excl. Labour)
DYFED	Shared Power		Shared Power

failed at the outset, as neither the Alliance nor the Conservative groups were prepared to concede the demand. Perhaps surprisingly, it succeeded for a time in Northumberland and in Avon.

The characteristic Conservative mistake was the precise reverse. Several Tory groups were prepared to form administrations *without securing any guarantees at all* from the other parties. This strategy, or lack of strategy, seemed almost to reflect an assumption that the Conservatives could continue to behave as the 'natural party of government' in the area. The realities of the new position soon imposed themselves, and these Conservative administrations found themselves being defeated over particular issues and then having to take public responsibility for carrying out policies of which they disapproved. Some fairly swift changes of strategy ensued in Cumbria, Oxfordshire, Leicestershire and Humberside.

The characteristic mistake of the Alliance parties in 1985 was to demand the sharing-out of committee chairs among all parties. Democratic though it may sound, this was not likely to be taken seriously by either of the other major parties, who viewed it as conclusive demonstration of Alliance naïvete and unsuitability for government.

All three parties soon learned from their mistakes. Later negotiations were generally underpinned by more realistic assumptions. The most interesting feature of the changes depicted in Table 13.2 is the number of counties which moved from 'minority administration' to 'no administration' (five counties) or 'shared power' (two counties). Both changes reflected a recognition by one or more parties that minority administration gave an illusion of power and was not worth continuing.

Put another way, it signified a growing appreciation of perhaps the most significant institutional characteristic of British local government: formal executive authority is located in the *full council*, rather than in a separate political executive. There is no equivalent of a cabinet of ministers at local level. As Colin Mellors puts it:

> Unlike some other local governments, and in contrast to national systems, there is no executive group which acts as the key prize for coalition bargains ... Committee chairmen in hung authorities have no executive power and are often able to do little more than control the proceedings of committee meetings. Without a voting majority on the committee, the value of their committee chairmanships is greatly

reduced and, indeed, may be considered so small as to be of no real value.[4]

Once the constraints and potential political costs of the hung situation are appreciated, the focus of inter-party negotiation tends to shift from the executive to what might be termed the legislative arena, and to the securing of votes on key policy issues. The way is open for the abandonment of minority administration and of any attempt to simulate majority control, and for the adoption of some system of rotating, *ad hoc*, or technical chairs.

This last term was coined to describe the nature of the agreement concluded by the parties on Cambridgeshire County Council. Initially, the Alliance had been allowed, with Labour support, to form a minority administration. But the Labour group became increasingly uneasy about the Alliance using the arrangement to gain public credit for what they felt were Labour initiatives. They therefore engineered a transition to a model of 'no administration' with 'technical chairs' shared out among all three groups. Peter Kellner explained:

> Traditionally, where one party controls a council, councillors who chair committees have considerable executive power, roughly analagous to cabinet ministers. 'Technical chairs' are more like the Speaker of the House of Commons: their sole job is to chair each meeting.[5]

The Emergence of Spokespersons

Directly related to the reduced role of committee chairs on hung authorities has been the enhanced role of party spokespersons. As committee chairs have become, to use Bagehot's famous distinction, one of the 'dignified' or ceremonial elements of the local government constitution, their place as one of the 'efficient' elements has been filled by party spokespersons.

In Cambridgeshire, for instance, a formal differentiation was made between the two roles and, to reduce the potential for conflict, spokespersons were not regarded as candidates for the post of committee chair. A similar principle was operated, in more acrimonious circumstances, in the London borough of Hillingdon between 1986 and 1990, where the mayor or deputy mayor chaired all committees. Except in hung authorities where one party is allowed to dominate by one or more of the others, this emphasis on spokespersons is much more congruent with the reality of the hung situation than any other approach.

The Growth of Informal Co-operation

The initial stance of Labour and Conservative parties on newly hung county councils was frequently headlined in the local press as 'No deals, no pacts, no coalitions'. The 'no coalitions' arm of the trinity held firm over the four-year period. What one might term 'formal executive coalitions' – in which two or more parties agree to form a joint administration with chairs shared out on the basis of an explicit working agreement – have been rarer among British hung authorities than among their European counterparts (e.g. in Belgium, Denmark, Italy, the Netherlands and Spain) with separate political executives.

There have been exceptions, mainly outside the county councils: for example, between the Conservatives and Liberals in Hammersmith & Fulham, Rochdale, Walsall, and Wolverhampton; and in Grampian Region in Scotland, where negotiations produced an intriguing collective administration of Scottish Nationalists, Liberals and Independents. But these are best seen as exceptions that prove the rule: executive coalitions are likely to be seen as far less relevant to a hung council than to a hung Parliament.

At the *informal* level, the hung counties did see a variety of pacts and deals, although their being publicised was unusual. In a response to outside enquiries, their existence would often be denied. But faced with a four-year period of no overall control, informal groupings of party leaders and spokespersons emerged to give direction to the council. Informal party working groups, set up to address particular issues, also grew in numbers and influence.

The Development of Medium-term Planning

It is a widely shared apprehension, certainly among officers in newly hung authorities, that prospects for strategic or medium-term planning will be seriously diminished. This was not, though, what Warwickshire County Council found in practice. Their comprehensive survey of 'Planning and Review in County Councils With No Overall Political Control' concluded:

> Conventional wisdom suggests that the loss of overall political control makes it nigh on impossible for an authority to plan, and makes resource allocation even more difficult, because of a lack of clear

priorities ... the evidence from county councils does not suggest such a clear conclusion at all.

The report noted that in five counties – Cambridgeshire, Devon, Essex, Hampshire and Oxfordshire – planning and review processes established before the loss of overall control had continued in operation, and in no case had there been any reduction in effectiveness. Moreover, all thirteen of the remaining hung counties surveyed reported having experienced significant development of either their planning or their review processes (or both) in the period *since* the loss of majority party control.

There are, to be sure, hung authorities outside the shire counties where longer-term planning has proved more difficult. But it is still a noteworthy finding that the disappearance of single-party control, far from preventing planning processes, seems in some instances to have stimulated them.

More Structured Budget Processes

There tends to be similar foreboding about budget-making; with the fear of endless meetings, possibly accompanied by threats from the District Auditor, and an eleventh-hour one-party budget passed with perhaps a majority of councillors abstaining.

Nor is the foreboding groundless. In hung authorities with little behind-the-scenes negotiations between the parties, budget-making has proved an agonised and acrimonious experience. But, in the words of the advertising copy, it doesn't have to be like that. It depends largely on how much early groundwork the parties are prepared to do at least to clarify areas of potential agreement. A budget-fixing meeting focused on a limited number of specific areas of choice is much more likely to reach a satisfactory outcome (after a reasonably conducted debate of reasonable length) than one where three alternative budgets are tabled for the first time. Among the counties, Cheshire developed an apparently effective system along these lines, in which:

> An all-party budget sub-committee does much of the spadework, and narrows down the areas of disagreement *before* the crucial council debate. In addition a different officer from the County Treasurer's department is allocated to each party group to help them work up their budget proposals.[6]

Similar arrangements were developed in other hung counties, and by

1989 there were far fewer budgetary wars of attrition – and many more examples of genuine inter-party negotiation and compromise than just two or three years earlier.

Clearer Procedures

The ability of the hung counties to cope with the initial procedural uncertainty following the 1985 elections is well illustrated by the spread of 'conventions documents' to facilitate the operation of council business. The Cheshire Conventions, first introduced in the 1981-85 period, were singled out by the Government-appointed Widdicombe Committee as a model for all other councils, whether hung or not. It was the Committee's recommendation, subsequently endorsed by the Government, that: 'individual local authorities should draw up, and make publicly available, conventions setting out the working relationships between the political parties and between councillors and officers.'

As we noted in *Co-operation and Conflict*, conventions documents were introduced quite widely in the hung counties. We also found, though, surprisingly little explicit reference to them, once negotiated. It seemed that if they could be negotiated, they were not really needed; and if they were needed, they could not be negotiated.

REDUCING THE DEMOCRATIC DEFICIT

Each of these six changes reflects the capacity of politicians to come to terms with an unfamiliar situation; and to establish new procedures and new ways of working together across previously sacrosanct party boundaries. But there have been other benefits of hung councils.

In the conventional conduct of British local government – as in the affairs of the European Community – it is not difficult to identify a democratic deficit. Much of the blame is directed at our electoral system and at the substantial number of councils it produces under long-term one-party domination, extending in many places to effective one-party monopoly.

Tony Byrne has allocated almost half of all councils in Great Britain into one of these two categories:

- in 64 (13 per cent) 80 per cent or more seats were held by one party;
- in 173 (34 per cent) 60-80 per cent of seats were held by one party.[7]

Such situations produce styles and practices of decison-making not possible in hung authorities. In *Co-operation and Conflict* we identified several features of 'hung politics' which may constitute inroads into the local democratic deficit:

- the enhanced relevance of the formal council and committee meetings (which are open to public and press), since votes are not necessarily predetermined by a single-party majority;
- the greater importance of discussion between councillors of different parties, both inside and outside committee;
- a widening of the policy agenda, since no approach is ruled out simply because the administration rejects it;
- an opening-up of the policy-making process, since more than one party is involved;
- a clarification of procedures (e.g. backbench members' access to information and officers' briefings), which may previously have been left unclear.

In these and other ways, we suggested, the operations of hung councils could foster a more open and democratic form of local government than that typically found in majority-controlled authorities.

HUNG COUNCILS NOW LEGITIMATE

In general, these trends of adjustment and democratisation have continued since the county council elections of May 1989. As a result of those elections the number of arithmetically hung counties almost halved, from twenty-five to thirteen. But with several of these counties – such as Bedfordshire, Cheshire, Gloucestershire, Leicestershire, Shropshire, Avon, Cumbria, Oxfordshire, Wiltshire – remaining hung for at least a second four-year term, the inclination of all parties to 'make the system work' increased. In the first five of these counties, a hung council now represents 'normality', and they celebrated – if that is the right word – a decade of continuous 'hungness' in May 1991.

There have been further moves away from minority administration, except in those relatively few councils where there is clear and explicit support for a large minority party from a smaller one. In Solihull, the only metropolitan district which became hung in the 1991 elections (if one discounts the internal split within the Liverpool Labour Party), a 'shared chairs' solution was agreed among all parties concerned. This is a policy which has still not officially found favour with Labour HQ in Walworth Road. But presented – as in Shropshire between 1985 and 1989 – as an administrative convenience, or accident, rather than an embryonic coalition, it appears to have escaped serious rebuke.

The expanding common ground between Labour and Liberal Democrat groups over policy priorities and expenditure levels (which we noted in *Co-operation and Conflict*) seems generally to have increased, albeit with a number of exceptions. But insofar as much of it was rooted in a shared antipathy to Thatcherism, it is possible that this trend may have peaked. We may be in for a move back to the pattern of the mid-1980s, when local Alliance groups were more inclined to support minority Conservative administrations.

Perhaps the most significant overall change, though, has been the increased recognition and acceptance of hung authorities as a legitimate form of local government. They are no longer regarded as an aberration, but rather as just as likely (and just as manageable) as majority control. There is nowadays a much more 'matter of fact' quality about the response to becoming hung, even when it is for the first time.

THE DOG THAT DIDN'T BARK: ELECTORAL PACTS

We have talked exclusively so far about the nature and consequences of *post*-election negotiations among politicians and party groups. That leaves the curious equivalent of Sherlock Holmes' dog that didn't bark – the *pre*-election negotiations between parties. They are, after all, not uncommon in local government in many other European countries.

It can be hard enough in Britain to get local politicians to admit to cross-party agreements of any kind – let alone ones in advance of an election campaign. But there can be no serious doubt that pre-election deals *were* struck between and among various local non-Conservative parties in the run-up to the 1989 county council elections – even if they were only rarely acknowledged in public.

The conditions were very favourable for such pacts. There were as many as twenty-one of the thirty-nine English county councils in which the Conservatives needed fewer than a dozen extra seats to secure a majority. If the non-Conservative parties in each of the councils could prevent a small number of Conservative gains, they might be able to hang on to at least some measure of influence on policy.

The national Labour leadership recognised the temptation facing many of their local parties. Neil Kinnock officially condemned the idea of reciprocal seat-sharing arrangements with other non-Conservative parties. But Labour's Environment spokesman, Jack Cunningham, turned a Nelsonian blind eye – 'If local parties want to make deals, it is a matter for them. But there is no question of encouraging them.'[8]

There were plenty of officially encouraged and well publicised pacts between the Democrats (as they then were) and the SDP to protect each other's sitting councillors – e.g. in Devon, Nottinghamshire, North Yorkshire, Kent, Lincolnshire, Wiltshire, Northumberland and Cleveland. But in almost all these instances the broader objectives of any deal, namely defeating the Conservatives, could be largely nullified by the intervention of a Labour candidate. The most significant arrangements were always likely to be between the Democrats and Labour. And here we become more dependent on a mixture of gossip and circumstantial evidence.

SELECTIVE WITHDRAWALS

Some of the most interesting statistics concerning the 1989 English county council elections were available before a single vote had been cast – the numbers of seats contested by the principal parties (summarised in Table 13.3).

Table 13.3 English County Council Election Candidates, 1985 and 1989

	1985		1989		Change	
	No.	%	No.	%	No.	%
Major Party candidates						
Conservatives	2789	93	2852	95	+63	+2.3
Labour	2748	91	2624	87	−124	−4.7
Liberal/SLD	1487	83	2203	82	−32	−1.3
SDP	1001		253			
Total = 3005						

The Conservatives fought just about every seat they were able to, and even more than they had in 1985. By contrast, Labour contested significantly fewer than previously, and in no fewer than fourteen counties left their potential supporters in at least ten seats without a Labour candidate to vote for. Some of these counties constitute areas of traditional Labour weakness, where the local party may have found difficulty finding suitable candidates prepared to stand in a hopeless cause. But that seems unlikely to account for some of the largest increases in seats uncontested by Labour between 1985 and 1989: sixteen in Gloucestershire, fourteen in Shropshire, thirteen in Buckinghamshire, ten in Somerset, nine in Lincolnshire, eight in Oxfordshire, seven each in Warwickshire and Hereford & Worcester, and six in Wiltshire.

It seems conceivable that some of these withdrawals reflected a reluctance to challenge a Liberal Democrat with a seemingly better chance of defeating a Conservative opponent – or at least a preparedness not to pressgang anyone to stand for Labour in such circumstances. Moreover (see Table 13.2), six of these nine authorities had been hung since 1985, and in all of them there had been some measure of co-operation between Labour and the Liberal Democrats. In all six the only realistic prospect of Labour retaining any power or influence depended on the council remaining hung, a tempting incentive to maximise the chances of all non-Conservative candidates.

In some of the other hung counties Labour's position was rather different. In Avon, Cumbria, Humberside, Lancashire and Northumberland, for example, they themselves had been in majority control prior to 1985 and could reasonably hope to be so again in the near future. In others – e.g. Cambridgeshire, Essex and Hertfordshire – it appears the local party, notwithstanding the possible indirect rewards of selective withdrawal, decided to maximise its overall vote by contesting almost every seat possible.

If there were, in some counties, tactical Labour withdrawals, this does not in itself demonstrate the existence of even an informal electoral pact. It takes two to tango. It is interesting, therefore, to find that the Liberal Democrats too contested significantly fewer seats in several of these nine counties than had the Alliance parties in 1985: for example, eighteen fewer in Lincolnshire, fifteen fewer in Wiltshire, and eleven fewer in Hereford & Worcester. This is far from conclusive evidence of reciprocal deals, but enough to justify a closer examination!

POLITICAL ICE HOCKEY

Assuming – for the sake of hypothesis – there *had* been a few informal electoral deals between the major non-Conservative parties, how effective were they? Did the strategy work?

With the help of Rallings and Thrasher's volumes of English County Council election results for 1985 and 1989, we made ward-by-ward comparisons across a few promising counties. We looked for circumstantial evidence of successful inter-party agreements. We scored evidence on the lines of ice hockey, in which, unlike football, points are awarded not just for goals, but also for 'assists': moves or passes which result directly in goals being scored.

A goal in this context is the election of a non-Conservative councillor, and a successful 'assist' is where the election of a candidate of one non-Conservative party appears to have been brought about by the action of another. An example of an 'active assist' would be where the Liberal Democrats gained a seat from the Conservatives following the decision of the Labour Party not to contest a seat where they had fielded a candidate in 1985. If they had not fought the seat in 1985 and simply decided again not to intervene in 1989, it would qualify as a 'passive assist', successful if the seat was gained by the Liberal Democrats and unsuccessful if retained by the Conservatives. At the other end of the scoring scale, there is the 'own goal', the opposite of an 'assist'. An example would be where the Conservatives gained a seat from the Liberal Democrats following the intervention of Labour in a seat they had not previously contested.

Considering the evidence from a number of counties, any reciprocal withdrawal deals that might have existed appear to have been only marginally successful. In Wiltshire, for example, there were several 1989 withdrawals by both Labour and the Liberal Democrats in Conservative-held seats they had fought in 1985. But while the SLD did manage to gain two such seats where Labour withdrew, the Conservatives retained three – and the Conservatives also held all six seats where the SLD withdrew. Moreover, the Conservatives gained seven previously SLD/SDP seats in which Labour did *not* withdraw, and two additional seats where Labour intervened for the first time.

The verdict on Wiltshire? Two successful 'assists' were effectively cancelled out by two 'own goals'. The Conservatives' failure to regain overall control of the Council owed little to the less than triumphant outcome of any Labour/SLD electoral pact.

In Hereford & Worcester, there were no actual 'own goals', but there were plenty of missed opportunities which, if taken, could easily have deprived the Conservatives of the overall control they narrowly retained. There were several withdrawals by both Labour and the SLD, but not in the most crucial marginal seats. The Conservatives held all five seats where Labour withdrew; and of the seven in which the Democrats withdrew, only one was gained by Labour, a lone successful 'assist'. On the other hand, no fewer than ten seats from which neither party withdrew were retained by the Conservatives with less than 50 per cent of the vote.

The scope for pre-election pacts was, and is, enormous – as are the potential rewards. It seems certain that the potential was recognised by some local parties in the 1989 elections, and that some strictly unofficial agreements were concluded in an attempt to realise it. But most of these attempts failed: agreements which were made were too few and far between, and frequently in the wrong places anyway!

CENTRAL/LOCAL DIFFERENCES

A deep-rooted resistance to electoral pacts is one characteristic common to both local and national politics. But in most other respects the differences outweigh the similarities, and considerable caution is required before attempting to draw any serious parallels between hung local authorities and a hung Parliament.

The fundamental difference is that a local authority does not require an administration, since the council itself and the committees to which it delegates formal responsibility constitute the executive. The operation of central government does require an executive, the cabinet, which needs the support of Parliament but is separate from it.

So the 'no administration' approach developed by local councils is not an option for central government. Nor is it likely that the ministerial role could be diminished, with civil servants consulting spokespersons of more than one party on an equal basis. This suggests the formal coalition option would be more probable if hung Parliaments became the norm.

Local government officers are responsible to the council as a whole, and to councillors of all parties. Civil servants in national government are responsible to their minister personally and have no formal relationship with MPs outside the government, not even those in the government party. Local government officers can play a considerably more active and more genuinely independent role in the hung situation than civil servants, whose main responsibility would still be to whoever happened to be the minister.

There are other important differences. The Prime Minister's right to request a dissolution means there is no fixed term for a hung Parliament, and the threat to exercise this right is a vital part of the politics of the hung situation. And of course the issues dealt with by central government are of a different magnitude, imposing different constraints and pressures on the politicians involved. In all sorts of ways the stakes are higher.

NOTES

1 Throughout this chapter we use the term 'hung' rather than 'balanced' or 'non-majority' mainly because it is the shortest and most commonly used of the three terms. We apologise if in so doing we upset the sensibilities of anyone who may see the term as having negative overtones.

2 David Butler, *Governing Without a Majority*, Collins, London 1983.

3 Steve Leach and Chris Game, *Co-operation and Conflict*, Common Voice, London 1989.

4 Colin Mellors and Bert Pijnenburg (eds), *Political Parties and Coalitions in European Local Government*, Routledge, London 1989, pp74-5.

5 Peter Kellner, 'A Quiet Political Revolution', *Independent*, 20 March 1989.

6 Steve Leach and John Stewart, *The Changing Patterns of Hung Authorities*, Local Government Training Board, Luton 1987.

7 Tony Byrne, *Local Government in Britain*, 5th edition, Penguin, Harmondsworth 1990.

8 John Cunningham, quoted in *Daily Telegraph*, 14 February 1989.

14

AN A-Z OF ELECTORAL SYSTEMS

SIMON OSBORN

A is for 'arithmetical accident' and 'absurd'.

This is how Dr Michael Thrasher and Dr Colin Rallings of the *Local Government Chronicle* Elections Centre have described local election results.

In 1990 in Islington Labour won all but three of the seats with under half the votes, and in Richmond-on-Thames the Liberal Democrats won 92 per cent of the seats on only 46.4 per cent of the votes. In the 1987 local election in Bracknell Forest the Conservatives won 54 per cent of the votes and all 44 seats.

B is for 'bipartisan'.

This is how we used to describe the two major parties' support for the current voting system. But since October 1990, Labour have been examining the alternatives.

B is also for 'bizarre results'. In the 1929, 1951 and February 1974 general elections the 'winners' lost and the 'losers' won. In each of these general elections (see G) the front runners – Baldwin's Tories in 1929, Attlee's famous 1945 Labour Government and Edward Heath's Conservatives in 1974 – all won more votes than their opponents, but lost the election.

In 1929, Ramsay MacDonald formed the first Labour Government with twenty-seven more MPs than Baldwin's Conservatives – even though he had won 285,000 fewer votes.

In 1951, Clem Attlee's Labour Government was thrown out by Churchill's Conservatives even though Labour gained almost a quarter of a million more votes.

In the February 1974 'Who runs the country?' election the tables turned against the Tories. This time Edward Heath left Downing Street in the Pickfords van even though his Party had gained 226,000 votes more than Harold Wilson's victorious Labour Party.

C is for 'constituency link'.

A famous Westminster myth: every MP represents the voters in their constituency or 'patch' and has a mystical link with them via the electoral process. However, 283 parliamentarians in the 1987-92 Parliament were elected by fewer than half the voters in their constituency. Opinion polls tell us that only one out of ten voters ever contact their MP.

Our Euro-MPs also claim a direct link with their constituents, but a 1989 MORI poll commissioned by the Conservative group in the European Parliament revealed that only 8 per cent of the voters could name their MEP.

D is for 'democracy'.

Something we have had in this country for centuries, and which we preach to the rest of the world. None of the newly democratised eastern and central European states copied our famous First-Past-the-Post voting system.

E is for 'Euro-election'.

The 1989 elections to the European Parliament surprised all the pundits when over two million British voters turned to the Greens, giving them almost 15 per cent of the votes and the highest vote of any Green Party in Europe.

Their continental colleagues in Germany won 8.4 per cent of the vote and eight seats. In France *Les Verts* won 10.5 per cent of the vote and ten seats. But Britain's Greens are not to be found in the corridors of power in Brussels and Strasbourg. Britain's hundred-year-old voting system has left supporters of our newest and youngest political party without a single representative in the European Parliament.

F is for 'First-Past-the-Post' and 'fairness'.

The latter has absolutely nothing to do with the former. Is it fair that 7,341,633 voters are represented in Parliament by only twenty-two MPs? That's how many voted for the two Davids' old Alliance of the Social Democrat and Liberal Parties in 1987 – nearly a quarter of all voters backed them but they have had only 3.4 per cent of the seats.

Is it fair that almost one and a quarter million people backed Labour in the south of England and have only three MPs outside London? Over a quarter of a million people supported the Conservatives in each of the cities of Manchester, Liverpool, Newcastle, Glasgow and Bradford; yet they elected not a single Conservative MP between them.

G is for 'general election'.

These supposedly happen every four or five years when voters choose between competing parties challenging each other to form a new Government.

In fact these elections, far from being general, are decided by those who happen to live in the 100 or so marginal seats. The number of voters concerned is less than the number who voted in the 1832 election after the first Great Reform Act.

H is for Huntingdon.

A 'safe' (see S) Conservative seat represented by John Major. It is not surprising, though worrying, that only three members of John Major's first cabinet were returned for constituencies above the line from the river Severn to the Wash.

I is for Islwyn.

A 'safe' (see S) Labour seat represented by Neil Kinnock. Mr Kinnock's shadow cabinet elected in 1991 had only two members returned for constituencies south of the line from the Severn to the Wash.

J is for 'joke'.

The joke is that John Major's and Neil Kinnock's parliamentary parties claim to represent the interest of the whole of Britain. Because of the archaic electoral system they are both unable to gain seats on one side of this rather arbitrary divide. By what mandate do John Major's southern Conservatives speak for Scotland or Neil Kinnock's northern and urban Labour Party speak for the rural South West?

K is for Kent.

In the 1987 general election the Conservatives gained just over half the votes across the county and won all the seats.

L is for 'legitimacy'.

None of the thirteen British Governments elected since the Second World War has had the support of the majority of the voters in the election. No wonder Lord Hailsham, the former Conservative Lord Chancellor, described the UK's system as 'elective dictatorship'!

M is for 'minority' and 'majority'.

All of those thirteen postwar Governments were elected by a minority of voters. Margaret Thatcher's famous 1983 landslide 144-seat majority was achieved with under 43 per cent of the vote.

M is also for John McQuade, elected MP for Belfast North in 1979 with 27.6 per cent of the vote.

N is for 'no overall control' (NOC).

NOC is often thought of as the initials of the winning party on local election night. Even our decisive, and simple to understand, voting system can end up giving us continental chaos and coalition government on our councils. Funny thing is the streets continue to be cleaned, the schools open the next day and the pothole in the pavement round the corner still won't be filled.

O is for 'one person, one vote, one value'.

In 1987 there was an average of 36,597 Conservative voters in the UK for every Conservative MP; 43,798 Labour voters for every Labour MP; and 333,711 Alliance voters for each of the twenty-two Alliance MPs.

P is for 'proportional representation'.

A strange and extremely complicated system of voting for which apparently a PhD in psephology is required to understand. Voters in Italy, Germany, Ireland, Namibia and over 300 other countries are clever enough to vote in PR elections. Luckily Britain's voting system is very simple.

Q is for 'quotas'.

A way of ensuring that a political party selects a target number of women or people from under-represented ethnic groups. Labour have recently set a target of 40 per cent women for all their internal elections. Labour's women hope that four in ten of the Party's MPs will be women by the year 2000.

The problem is that almost 89 per cent of the current PLP are male, and that, on average, only twenty-nine of these have retired at the end of each of the last twelve Parliaments. If Labour selected women for all the seats of its retiring MPs it would take another four elections to reach the target. And besides, all the selection committees in those seats would have to choose women. Move over darling!

R is for Representation of the People Act.

The RPA governs the way we vote. Perhaps the Trades Descriptions laws should be used to change the name to something more appropriate.

S is for 'safe seats' and 'stable government'.

There are at least 544 'safe' seats in the UK. In a safe seat the result is almost a foregone conclusion – hence the phrase: 'You could put a donkey up here so long as it had the right rosette.'

The number of 'safe' seats has steadily increased since the War. Professors Curtice and Steed estimate that 76 per cent of seats in 1955 were 'safe', and that by 1987 87 per cent had become 'safe'.

It is claimed that First-Past-the-Post has created stable government. A recent Institute of Economic Affairs report, however, has pointed out that British cabinet ministers under both Labour and Conservatives are reshuffled more often than in most European governments elected under PR systems. Professor Finer pointed out in 1975 that most of PR-elected Europe had experienced fewer changes of prime minister than Britain.

During the 1970s the CBI mocked the idea of the stability of British government, calling it 'ping pong' politics: first one side nationalised the steel industry, then the other side privatised it, then Labour returned and nationalised, and eventually the Conservatives returned to privatise it – the history of one industry from 1951 to 1988.

T is for 'turnout'.

The numbers who vote in Britain reached an all-time high in 1951, when 83.9 per cent of the electorate polled. By 1987 the turnout had fallen to 75.3 per cent.

An analysis of the turnout has revealed that the Welsh avail themselves of their democratic right in greater numbers than any other part of the UK since 1922. The citizens of Northern Ireland tend to have the poorest record for voting except in European elections, when they turn out in much higher numbers than the rest of the UK.

In the first direct elections to the European Parliament in 1979 turnout in Northern Ireland was 22.3 per cent higher than the rest of the UK, in 1984 it was 29.6 per cent higher and in 1989 12.9 per cent higher. Northern Ireland uses PR when it votes in Euro-elections.

U is for 'uniform electoral system'.

The Treaties of Rome and Paris instruct the European Parliament to draw up a 'uniform electoral system' for Euro-elections. The latest report, which establishes proportional representation as the basis for future Euro-elections in Britain, was passed by the MEPs in October 1991 by 150 votes to twenty-six.

V is for 'vote'.

'A formal expression of one's opinion or choice' – the *Oxford English Dictionary*. And, under First-Past-the-Post, you are lucky if it is anything more than a mere formality (see W).

W is for 'wasted votes'.

In 1987 just over 32.5 million people voted in the general election. Although all the votes were counted, unfortunately 15,627,016 people voted for unsuccessful candidates. Tough luck?

X is for 'X voting'.

First-Past-the-Post predates both universal suffrage and the modern political parties. It comes from a time when the vast majority of voters were illiterate, and an 'X' helped them express an opinion.

Y is for 'young voters'.

Attempts to change our voting system are always titanic struggles against strong opposition, followed by legislation and subsequent wide acceptance.

Reducing the voting age from twenty-one to eighteen was fiercely opposed, but this most recent electoral reform bill was finally passed in 1969, adding almost four million new voters to the electorate for the 1970 general election. Who now would think of removing these young voters from the register?

Z is for 'zealot'.

A name for people who want to change our voting system, usually given to them by politicians elected by First-Past-the-Post.

NOTES ON CONTRIBUTORS

Sarah Benton is lecturer in American politics, Birkbeck College, University of London.

Helena Catt is lecturer in politics, University of Auckland.

Tim Dawson, formerly assistant editor at *Marxism Today*, is now a freelance journalist.

Nina Fishman is senior lecturer in history and politics, Harrow College, Polytechnic of Central London.

Chris Game is a lecturer, Institute of Local Government Studies, University of Birmingham.

Peter Hain is Labour MP for Neath.

Peter Hanington is a freelance journalist.

Peter Jones is Scottish Political Editor of *The Scotsman*.

Anna Kruthoffer is co-ordinator of the Electoral Reform Society's 'Democracy 2000' campaign for women's representation.

Steve Leach is senior lecturer, Institute of Local Government Studies, University of Birmingham.

David Marquand is professor of politics, University of Sheffield.

David Martin is Labour Member of the European Parliament for Lothians.

Simon Osborn is campaigns manager of the Electoral Reform Society.

Jeff Rooker is Labour MP for Birmingham Perry Barr.

Gareth Smyth edited *Can The Tories Lose? The Battle for the Marginals*, (Lawrence & Wishart, 1991), and has written on electoral reform in various publications.

Robin Squire is Conservative MP for Hornchurch.

INDEX

ABOUT COMMON VOICE

Operating from a centre-left perspective, **Common Voice** exists to encourage debate and discussion across the political spectrum.

Common Voice has published or co-published:

The Intelligent Person's Guide to Electoral Reform, by Helena Catt.
Co-operation and Conflict: Politics in the Hung Counties, by Steve Leach and Chris Game.
Can the Tories Lose? The Battle for the Marginals, edited by Gareth Smyth.

Common Voice can be contacted at 6 Chancel Street, London SE1 0UU.